MARY BARATTA-LORTON

WORKJOBS ACTIVITY-CENTERED LEARNING FOR EARLY CHILDHOOD EDUCATION

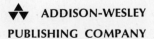 ADDISON-WESLEY
PUBLISHING COMPANY

Menlo Park, California • Reading, Massachusetts
London • Don Mills, Ontario

This book is in the
ADDISON-WESLEY INNOVATIVE SERIES

Photographs by William Skeahan

ISBN 0–201–04311–4
33 34 35 36 37 38 39-WC-05 04 03 02 01 00 99

Contents

Classification   67

Sounds and Letters   109

THE DEVELOPMENT OF MATHEMATICS
THROUGH WORKJOBS   127

Sets   129

Number Sequences   181

Combining and Separating Groups 193

Relationships 213

ACTIVITY-CENTERED LEARNING:
WHY AND HOW 239

INDEX TO SKILLS 253

WORKJOBS

During my years of teaching I have made learning tasks for the children in my classes in the form of manipulative activities built around a single concept. My idea was that through active involvement with the materials the child would draw out the generalizations within the material. Through conversation with me, the teacher, the child would have the opportunity to express something about his experience and I would have the opportunity to ask him questions to help him become aware of patterns and relationships he intuitively observed but could not yet clearly define.

The children called the activities their "work" or their "jobs." One day a child put the words together as a joke—and it stuck.

M.B.L.

WORKJOBS IN ACTION: A GLIMPSE

Patricia has on a paper mailman's hat and is taking a letter from the mail pouch around her shoulder. She carefully scans the 14 paper houses placed on the table in front of her for the house number that matches the address on the letter. The fifth house number is a match—Patricia smiles and places the letter on top of the house. In a very businesslike way, she takes the next letter from the mail pouch and begins scanning the 14 paper houses for their numbers so she may "deliver" the letter.

David is working on the floor with the cars and garages. He is counting the number of dots on a small toy car. "One, two, three, four, five." David looks among the garages for the one with the number 5. "Ruhnnn!" Into the garage with the number 5 on top goes the car. David takes the next car and begins to count its dots. "One, two, three . . ."

Lisa is working nearby with the hook board. She is sorting the small, medium, and large metal washers onto the small, medium, and large hooks. She has nearly finished but is having trouble. There are two large washers left in her hand but there is one large and one medium hook left on the board. Lisa seems very perplexed. She looks back at the hook board, fingers the medium hook, and looks down at the large washer. Then she begins systematically checking the other washers on the board. After several minutes Lisa laughs and removes a medium washer from a large hook where she had placed it earlier, and puts the

3

medium washer there and the two large washers on the two remaining large hooks. With a squeal of delight Lisa jumps up and goes to the teacher saying, "I did it! Come and see." The teacher is working with John at the pocket chart but says she will be right there.

John has the color cards at the top of the pocket chart (red, black, yellow, blue, green, white, brown, gray, and orange) and is sorting black and white pictures of various objects under their appropriate color. The teacher is asking John, "What is this a picture of?" John answers confidently, "A snowman." The teacher asks, "If you were playing in the snow and made a snowman, what color would he be?" John points to the white color card at the top of the pocket chart and answers, "White." "Very good, John. Where will you put this picture, then?" He places it under the white color card. John takes the next picture, a fire engine, and indicates that it would be placed under the red color card; he then places it there. The teacher compliments John on his work and reminds him to let her know when he finishes. Now the teacher goes to see Lisa's work at the hook board.

"What a fine job you've done. Tell me about it."

Lisa explains: "I put the little rings on the little hooks, the big ones on the big hooks, and this kind-a-ones, here."

Indicating the size Lisa just described, the teacher asks her, "And what size could you call this one?"

Lisa thinks a moment and says, "I don't know, but it's like Mama bear in *The Three Bears* story!"

The teacher smiles and says, "Yes, it is, isn't it? Mama bear is not as big as Papa bear and not as small as Baby bear—she's in the middle. Now, what could you call this size ring if it's like Mama bear?"

Lisa shrugs and says, "I guess we could say it's middle-sized too!"

They laugh together and then the teacher asks, "How many middle-sized rings are there?" Lisa begins to count . . .

Patricia has finished the mailman game and now is working over by the sink with the rice game. She is measuring rice through a funnel into various sizes of glass jars. Some are short and squat, some are tall and thin. Some have curved sides, others have straight ones. Patricia is humming and occasionally she talks to herself saying, "Just a little bit more . . . okay . . . STOP!" She smiles when she reaches the rubber band that is glued at a particular level on each jar. Sometimes Patricia goes over the mark slightly and stops humming, frowns, and says, "Too much!" or "Goooooo back!" She then removes some of the rice and fills the jar more slowly than before, stopping exactly at the marker.

Robert is dropping beans into old vitamin bottles according to the number on each bottle. "One, two, three, four, five, six, seven, eight, nine." He puts the top on the bottle and takes another.

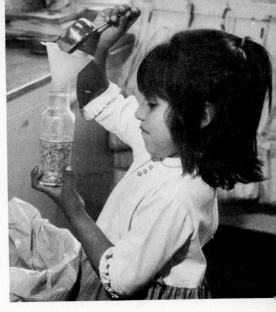

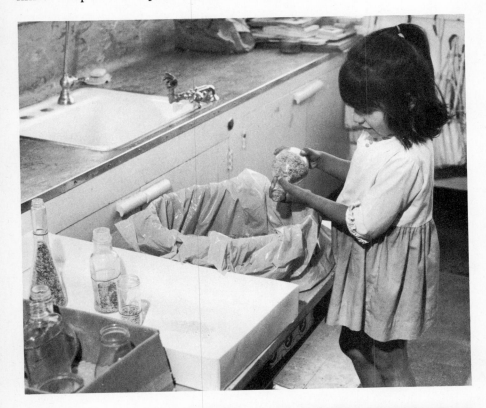

The teacher is checking Amalia's pegboards and is pointing to the model which has been reproduced. She asks Amalia if the pattern is the same as the model. Amalia quickly removes two purple pegs in the yellow area and replaces them with yellow pegs.

Near the front of the room John and David are working with the height-measuring game. John has measured David and says he is 3 feet and 13 inches tall. David says yes, but that he thinks John should trade 12 of the little blocks for one more long block. John agrees and makes the exchange. He puts on the fourth long block and then the one little block. John checks to be sure the measurement is correct then calls Valerie, a fifth-grade assistant, over to check his work. Valerie helps John record David's height on the clipboard and asks him who was taller: Mike, the first person he measured, or David, the second.

The teacher is working with Rudy at the other side of the room. He has been arranging several pictures to tell a story and is explaining to the teacher the rationale for his arrangement. "I put this picture first because first the telephone rings up. This one is next because the lady is talking on the phone. At the end she hangs up and goes away because she's done talking." The teacher selects a sequence that she finds questionably arranged and asks Rudy to tell her about it. He explains how the first picture shows the people leaving the house to go on a picnic. The second picture shows they forgot something and have to go back inside to get what was forgotten. Last of all, they arrive at the picnic spot and eat their lunch. The teacher is obviously surprised at Rudy's story for she had been looking at it another way. She smiles and explains that she thought his explanation and arrangement very interesting. She had thought the second picture would go at the end, showing the people when they returned home after the picnic was over. Certainly, though, she could see it Rudy's way too! They discuss another sequence together, and then the teacher goes to see John, who has been waiting to show her his activity.

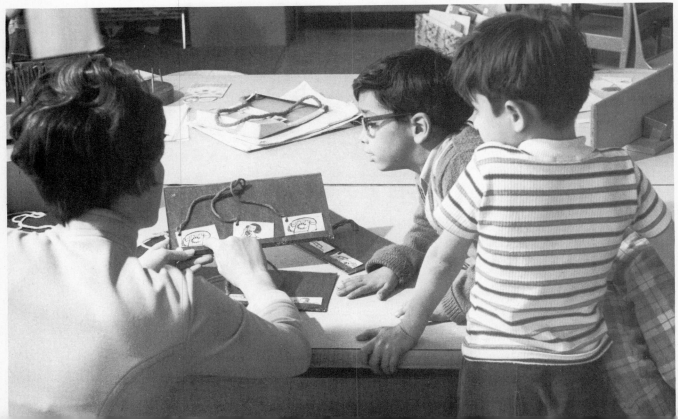

Antoinette has been working at the back of the room in a cubbyhole behind the teacher's desk. She has finished matching plastic letters from her name to an alphabet strip and tells the teacher with surprise, "Look! I have five *t*s." Together they go to Antoinette's desk and examine her name card to verify this. They find three *t*s in her first name and two in her last. The teacher asks her if she has a lot of any other letter in her name. "Yes," she responds, "four *e*s and two *o*s and three *n*s—see!" The teacher notices the letter *g* from her last name has not been placed on the alphabet strip and asks Antoinette about it. "I didn't know where to put it." The teacher places it under the letter *a* and asks, "Is this the same letter?" Then she places it under the letter *c* and asks again, "Is this the same letter?" She continues this questioning until Antoinette sees the *g* and takes the letter from her hand and places it over the letter *g* on the alphabet strip. Then she asks Antoinette to point to some of the letters as she names them: *y, m, c, j,* . . .

Noemi and Karla are at the workshelf selecting their next activity. Tommy is working with the flannelboard putting up body parts so they fit together to form a body. Elizabeth is working on the language board hanging up pictures of boys and girls and matching the words *boy* and *girl* to the pictures. Jimmy is finding the two cans that sound alike when he shakes them and is placing them in pairs on the answerboards. Eric is sitting at the side table trying to pair various squares of textured materials while blindfolded.

In the middle of the room, Anthony and Leticia are waiting for the teacher's assistant to see their work. Valerie, the assistant, tells Leticia, "Sit by your work until I talk with Anthony—then I'll come to see you." Anthony has been attempting to reproduce a series of pegboard patterns. Valerie, pointing to an incorrectly matched pattern, asks, "Anthony, is this pattern exactly the same as the model?" Anthony studies his pattern and the model. Noticing the error, he answers, "Nope," and immediately begins to remove the incorrectly matched pegs. Valerie leaves Anthony to finish this and goes to see Leticia's work.

Leticia has been working at the table with the puzzle pieces that form geometric shapes. Valerie checks Leticia off on her recording sheet and then talks with her about the circle not yet fit together. Leticia works turning the pieces around and over until she gets them to fit correctly.

Rhonda has been working on the floor near the window with the pincushion game. Walking by, the teacher notices immediately that it has been done perfectly. Five pins are in the pincushion with the number 5. Seven pins are in the one with the number 7. Ten pins are in the pincushion with the number 10, and so forth. She compliments Rhonda on what a good job she is doing and how carefully she is working. Two children working nearby show the teacher how they have lined their work up in numerical order—number 1 first, then number 2, then number 3, and so on. The teacher is obviously pleased and talks with them for a moment.

Valerie is complimenting Anthony's work with the pegboard patterns, which he has now corrected. Soon she goes to the far corner of the room to see another child who has just finished.

At the side table Lisa is working with the rice game, filling each jar to the rubber band mark. Moses is nearby "delivering the mail" to the paper houses. Olivia is on the rug shaking the sound cans and placing the pairs together. Nearby, Gina is hanging cherries on the plastic trees according to the number indicated on each tree. Pamela is recording the number of nails the rubber band is around in each row.

Patricia is sorting pictures of people of all ages according to whether they are working or playing. Robert is sorting cards on the floor into two piles. Each card has two pictures on it. If they are both the same, Robert puts the card on the answerboard that says "same." If they are different, he puts the card on the answerboard that says "different."

The teacher is talking with John very near where Robert is working. "And why did you put this picture (a black and white drawing of some bananas) under this color (green), John?" The child answers unhesitatingly, "Because Mama always buys them when they're green so they last longer." The teacher smiles and compliments John on his interesting way of looking at it. The teacher now indicates a picture of a polar bear, which is under the brown color card along with a nest, some wood, and a brown bear. She suggests to John that he go to the library shelf and look in a particular animal book (with which he is familiar) and find a picture of a polar bear. John goes to the shelf to do this and the teacher goes to help the next child who is ready.

On the way to see the next child's work, the teacher notices that Garvin is not working. She goes up to him and asks what the matter is. Garvin says, "It's too hard! I can't do it." The teacher, who knows Garvin is able to do this work, encourages him. He still insists he doesn't want to do the work because it's too hard, so the teacher kneels down beside him and asks him if he saw Gayle Sayers play football on the TV over the weekend. "Do you know how he got to be a football star—such a good one? Well, there were many times when the coach told him to run down to the end of the field when all he wanted to do was give up. What he really wanted to do was just sit down! 'I'm too tired,' he'd think. 'It's too hard!' Then he'd think some more about it and realize, 'Yeah, it's hard, but I want to be good, and to be a good football player I know I have to do the hard stuff too'." The teacher asks Garvin, "Do you want to learn and be good at your work—really good?" Garvin hesitatingly says, "Yes." The teacher then tells him, "When you're really learning, sometimes it's going to be hard and you'll want to quit. You can say 'it's hard'—that's okay. We all understand when it's hard, but there's one thing you can't say—you can't say, 'I can't.' If it's tough, you have to keep on trying, a little at a time, and don't give up. Remember Gayle Sayers doesn't give up when it's tough. He doesn't do only the easy stuff. He keeps at the hard work because he knows it will help him make touchdowns. If you keep at the hard work, you'll soon be able to do the work and when you're finished, do you know what? Then you'll think it's easy." Pointing to his work, the teacher asks if he is willing to try again. Looking much encouraged, Garvin says "Yes." He takes the five pictures that the teacher holds out to him and begins to work. The teacher tells him she will go to see some of the children's work and then will stop back to see how he's doing.

John has now found the picture of the polar bear in a book at the bookshelf. He studies the picture intently. After awhile he goes back to his work and moves the polar bear's picture from under the brown color card to under the white. On the way to check Patricia, the teacher notices Garvin has the five cards sorted that she had given to him. "Wow!" she says, "You didn't give up, Garvin! Good for you. You finished your work just like Gayle Sayers would have." Garvin smiles and the teacher gives him five more cards to sort and says, "Try this new pile of cards and I'll stop back again in a few minutes." Valerie is working at the table at the far side of the room with Carl, a boy who has just entered the class that day. She realizes immediately that Carl has chosen a workjob that is far too difficult for him. He has used no logic with this task and she does not have the time now to stay with him and explain every step. Valerie says to the child, "That's fine, Carl. Let me help you put this workjob away and then we'll find something for you to try next." They go together to the workshelf where three other children are busy putting away the work they have just finished or selecting the task they are going to do next. The assistant selects two activities, both of which will assure Carl's success on his first day in class. He chooses one of the activities and the assistant watches while he begins. She encourages his efforts and then goes to the next child who is waiting for her.

Ronald is counting out the Cocoa Puffs into the vitamin pill bottles. "One, two, three, four, five, six, . . ." John is now driving cars into the garages. Karla is walking over to a place behind the work cupboard with the hook board and the metal washers. She sits down and dumps out the washers onto the rug and begins to place them on the hooks. Eric is putting away the pegboard game on the workshelf.

Gina is sorting pictures of animals into piles of those which live mainly on land, those which live mainly in the water, and those which fly in the air. She sorts pictures for several minutes. When she comes to the picture of the hippopotamus she looks around for the teacher. She sees Patricia and the teacher are engrossed in conversation at the other side of the room so she turns to Vincent working nearby and shows him the picture and asks, "What is this?" Vincent proudly tells her, "It's a hippopotamus." They talk together about where they might see a hippopotamus. Vincent tells how his grandfather took him to the zoo last summer and he remembers seeing a hippopotamus in a big tank of water. Gina still seems puzzled and says, "Well, he goes into the water, but sometimes he can come out and walk around—I remember that on TV—so, could I put him in the middle, between the land and the water?" Vincent smiles and says, "Why not?"

Patricia is explaining why she sorted the picture of a man's pipe into the slot near the man's waist on the big drawing of a man's body. "How does a man use a pipe here?" asks the teacher. Patricia explains how her uncle always carries his pipe in his pocket. "I wouldn't have thought of that!" remarks the teacher with a smile. "And what about this picture of a ring in the slot on the man's head?" Patricia laughs and quickly removes the ring from that slot and shifts it down to a slot near the hand. The teacher checks through the remaining cards, shuffles them, and gives them to Patricia to put away.

Valerie is sitting on the floor beside Alicia discussing her work with the button-sorting game. They stop their conversation momentarily to listen to the teacher talking to Garvin about the work he has just finished. "Is this the same guy who wanted to give up and do only the easy work? Look, everyone, Garvin really stuck to his job! He didn't

say, 'I can't,' when it was hard—and now look, he's finished his work by himself!" Garvin looks very proud and tries to pass all the attention off by saying to his friend standing near by, "Aw, this is easy! Do you want to try it next?"

The teacher is now at the front of the room discussing the measuring game with Lisa and Eric. Rudy is working on the sequence cards by the front blackboard and is lining them up very carefully as he finishes. Kenneth is working with the pincushions and counting out the pins. Tommy is hanging up the clothes on the clothesline in numerical order. He seems to be having some difficulty with which number to put next, but he looks at the workshelf and then goes to get one of the number cards which are in a folder taped to the side. Antoinette is at the back table looking for the number 4605 on the paper houses to match that number on her envelope.

The teacher is sitting with James who has placed the train cars in the following order: 1 2 3 4 5 6 8 9 7 10. The teacher removes the last four cars and says, "Tell me which cars are lined up, James." She points to the cars one at a time, as he counts, "One, two, three, four, five, six." "Good, says the teacher. "Now, what number comes next?" James gets the car and says, "Seven." He continues to link the other cars in order up to ten. The teacher compliments him on his good work and goes to see Antoinette's mailman game at the back table.

Antoinette has matched the envelopes to the houses. All but two are correctly matched. The letter which was supposed to be delivered to 6405 was delivered to 6450. The teacher picks up these two envelopes from the houses and says, "Show me where these two go, will you please?" Antoinette goes about matching the numbers in her own way but ends up with the same result—6405 is matched with 6450 and vice versa. The teacher again picks up the envelopes and says, "Let's do it together this time. Read this number with me, Antoinette." They read

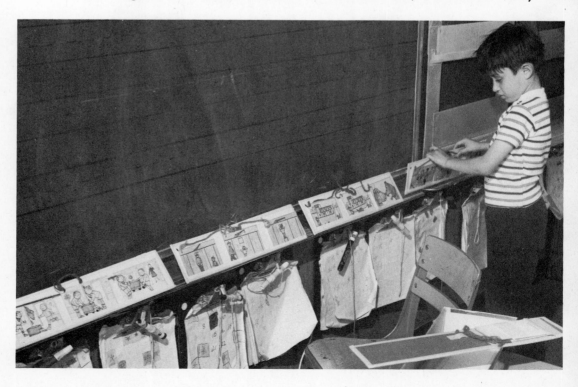

number 6405 together. Then they go to the first house (6450) and the teacher and Antoinette read that number together. The teacher asks her, "Are these two numbers the same?" Antoinette checks each number slowly and finds they are not exactly the same. Then they go to the other house and read its number. She quickly sees that this is the number she is looking for and places the envelope on top of the house. The teacher compliments her on looking carefully at the order of the numbers and says, "You didn't let a tricky number fool you, Antoinette! You've done a very good job."

The teacher glances up at the clock and notices it is almost time for lunch. She calls for the class's attention and points out the time to them. She reminds the children not to choose another activity. When the activity they are now doing is finished and checked, they may get a book from the library shelf and sit down on the rug. Two children who were on their way to the workshelf to get their next activity go instead to the library shelf, get a book, and sit down on the rug. The teacher looks up from where she is working and compliments these two children for following her directions. Overhearing this, two other children, who had stopped to watch their friend complete his activity, hurry to the library shelf to get a book and then join their friends on the rug.

The teacher and Valerie continue working with the children. As each child finishes talking with the teacher, he puts his work back into its container and returns it to the workshelf before going to the library shelf for a book. When most of the children have finished, the teacher leaves her assistant to help those not yet through. She goes to the rug and compliments the children who are there for the wonderful way they worked during the work period. She is really pleased, for they worked so hard and learned so much. She compliments several individual children for what they did today. She smiles at Garvin and praises him especially, because today Garvin learned to say "I can" instead of "I can't."

THE DEVELOPMENT OF LANGUAGE THROUGH WORKJOBS

At different times during the morning workperiod, several children, in succession, may select the same activity, such as the bolt board. Even though each child will perform the same task—i.e., screwing the bolts into the nuts glued to the board by fitting the three different size bolts to their matching nuts—there is a great difference in the children's ability to express this experience in words. For example, one child might be able to explain his work in the following way: "I was working with these metal things glued onto this long board. I screwed the long things into the metal pieces on the board. Some of them were small ones and some were big and some were in between. I could screw them together because they have these raised-up lines on the metal parts that make them fit together." A second child, on the other hand, may only be able to say, "Uhh . . . I filled up the holes," and will stare in silence and shrug when asked how he went about it.

Because children come to school in all stages of readiness, they have different abilities and different needs. The first child who explained his work with the bolt board needs his teacher to help him mainly with vocabulary—"bolt" for "long thing," "nut" for "metal piece," and "thread" for "raised-up lines." The second child needs far more from his teacher. He needs help in clarifying his thinking: in naming the objects he used, in expressing the actions he performed, in identifying the colors or materials or shapes of the objects, in seeing relationships, and in gaining facility in expressing his thinking in words. Clearly, the

17

teacher can only touch on a few of these areas in the brief period of time she will spend with this child when he has completed his activity, but it is in this conversation that the teacher begins to meet each child's need for language development.

The child may not express himself clearly and precisely on *this* occasion, but certainly he will make gains. The accumulated confidence and skill which this child, and others like him, gain by going one step at a time does lead to clearer and more confident self-expression. This discussion between the teacher and the child at the completion of each activity is crucial: it provides the opportunity, the need, for each child to express himself in language. Unless the teacher creates this opportunity, through her questions, a child who does not have the verbal facility to express himself clearly will have no reason to attempt to organize his thinking and express his thoughts in words.

Each teacher will find the basis for her questions for follow-up discussion after each activity primarily from the child she is working with. The child who needs to increase his vocabulary will be helped to learn new words. The child who needs a review of his colors will get it. The child who wants to learn to write all the words in a workjob will be given the opportunity. And the child who has difficulty expressing even the simplest thought will be helped step by step to confident expression.

Ideas for follow-up discussions are given for each workjob. With one child a teacher may have the opportunity to cover all the skills and questions for a particular workjob. With another she may use only one or two. And with still others, because she is following the child's cues, she may find the listed possibilities not appropriate at all. The importance of the follow-up discussions doesn't lie in the particular question asked; rather, it is the opportunity afforded each child to verbalize his experiences and be able to put his thoughts into words.

Perception

Sequences

Skills Interpreting pictures and details; developing logical thinking; strengthening left-to-right progression; placing a series of pictured events in sequence to tell a story.

The child looks through the pictures. He decides what he thinks happened in the story and places the first picture in the sequence at the left. The next picture will show the second event, and so forth, until the story is told. The child repeats this procedure for each pocket chart story in the workjob.

The teacher might assist the child to begin by saying, "Look at all the pictures and see if you can guess what happened first—put that picture by the dot [or X] here at the left. Put what happened next here; and what happened at the end will go—where? Yes, now do the first one while I watch."

Tell me about this story.
Which picture happened last in the story about the man with a flat tire on his car?
Which picture happened first in this story?
What are the people wearing in the story about the cat?
How do you think the people feel in this story? Why do you think they feel this way?
How many stories did you arrange in order?
Which story did you like best? Which was the funniest? Why did you think it was funny?

A group of pictures that tell a story when placed in order.
A small pocket chart for each set of pictures made by stapling a 1/2″ strip along the bottom of a tagboard rectangle.
Yarn or elastic tied through a hole in each picture and then secured to the individual pocket chart.
Spray paint to paint pocket charts.
Library-book pocket glued to the back of each pocket chart to hold pictures between uses.
Container for the pocket charts.

Note: It is helpful to mark an X or a dot at the left of each pocket chart to indicate the correct position for the first picture in each series.

The Rice Game

The child pours the rice into the jars, being careful to stop filling each jar at the line marked by the rubber band.

Some children will enjoy counting the number of scoops of rice it takes to fill each jar. They can record the number of scoops on a small piece of paper placed in front of each jar. After all the jars are filled the child might order them from the one containing the least amount of rice to the one with the most.

The teacher might say, "See if you can fill the jars up to the line exactly!"

Tell me about your work, Janice.
What exactly did you do?
Which jar do you think has the most rice in it? The least? What makes you think so?
Are there any jars that have the same amount of rice?
What color rubber band is on the jar that is half full?
Do you remember which jar was the first one you filled? The last one?
What do we call this food?
Do you ever have it at home? Who fixes it?
Pour the rice out of this bottle and find out how many cups there are.
Would you like to do it for these others, and write down how many cups you used in all? How would you go about it?

Assorted glass jars and bottles (about ten) of varying sizes and shapes.
Colored rubber bands glued to different levels on the containers.
2 to 6 lb of rice, depending on the size of the jars and bottles used.
Plastic dishpan for the rice.
Funnel.
Scoop or long-handled measuring cup.
Container for jars.

Note: It also is a good idea to place the lid of a large box (as a blanket box) under the jars to catch spills. Have the child fill the jars *in* the dishpan and then set them aside.

The teacher may want to vary the rice game at some time during the year by coloring some of the rice. This can be done by shaking a cup of rice in a jar along with 1½ tablespoons of rubbing alcohol and a squirt of food coloring.

Jars and Lids

The child puts the lids on the jars. The task is self-checking: there are twelve jars and twelve lids. If the child puts the wrong lid on one of the jars, he will have a lid left at the end that does not fit the remaining jar.

Children enjoy timing themselves with a stopwatch to see how long it takes them to replace all the lids on the jars. A child can keep track of his best time and compete with himself to improve his time.

Children also enjoy measuring around the widest part of the jar with a piece of string and comparing this length to the jar's height.

The teacher might say to the child, "Can you put these together?"

Antoinette, look at this lid for a minute. Do you think it could fit on this jar? Why not? Do you think this one is too small too? How about this one? Try it and see. Good!

Show me a lid that you think would be much too small for this jar. Show me one you think would be much too big. Now show me one you think would be just about right.

Show me the jar with the biggest lid. Well, that's the biggest *jar* for sure, but which jar has the biggest *lid?*

Which jar has the smallest lid?

Show me how you put on this lid. What do we call that motion? What about if you take it off? What do we call the motion?

How many jars are there? How many lids? Are there more jars than lids?

What are these jars made of? What are the lids made of?

GETTING STARTED

IDEAS FOR
FOLLOW-UP DISCUSSION

MATERIALS

Twelve jars with lids, each of a different circumference.
Container for the lids.
Container for the boxed lids and the empty bottles.

Corks

Skills Distinguishing between different sizes and using this skill to make predictions; experiencing one-to-one correspondence; developing the visual and tactile senses; experiencing success in completing a task.

The child takes the corks and rubber tips and fits them together. The **ACTIVITY**
task is self-checking since the child must do it correctly or he will have
corks left over that do not fit into rubber tips. After placing the corks
and rubber tips together, the child can group them together in some
way.

Children for whom this task would be very easy may enjoy trying it
blindfolded.

Other children may enjoy estimating the length of all the pairs placed
in a line by cutting a length of string and then placing the pairs in a line
to check the estimation. They might also estimate the height of the
pairs stacked one on top of the other and then check this prediction.

The teacher might begin with: "What can you do with these two
things? Show me. Good! I'd like to see them when they're all put
together."

GETTING STARTED

How are these things the same? Is there anything different about them?

IDEAS FOR
FOLLOW-UP DISCUSSION

How many sizes are there? Show me a small cork. A small rubber tip.
  Show me a large cork. A large rubber tip.
Put this cork into the rubber tip you think it fits. And this one.
What did you do with the corks?
Show me a small cork and rubber tip. Are there any more small sets?
  How many? How many is that altogether?
Show me a large set. Show me three large sets.
Are there any sets that are the same in some way that you could group
  together? How are these the same? Yes, they're the same size! Can
  you group all the sizes together?

MATERIALS

Seven small corks and nonskid chair leg tips to fit the corks.
Seven medium corks and tips.
Seven large corks and tips.
Bucket (3-quart size) or other suitable container for the separated corks and tips.

Note: If rubber chair leg tips are used, they may be cut down about 1/2″ with a
serrated knife so the child can more easily push in and remove the corks.

Button It Up

Skills Developing small-muscle and hand-eye coordination; learning skills for dressing and undressing; to snap, button, hook, zip, tie, and buckle.

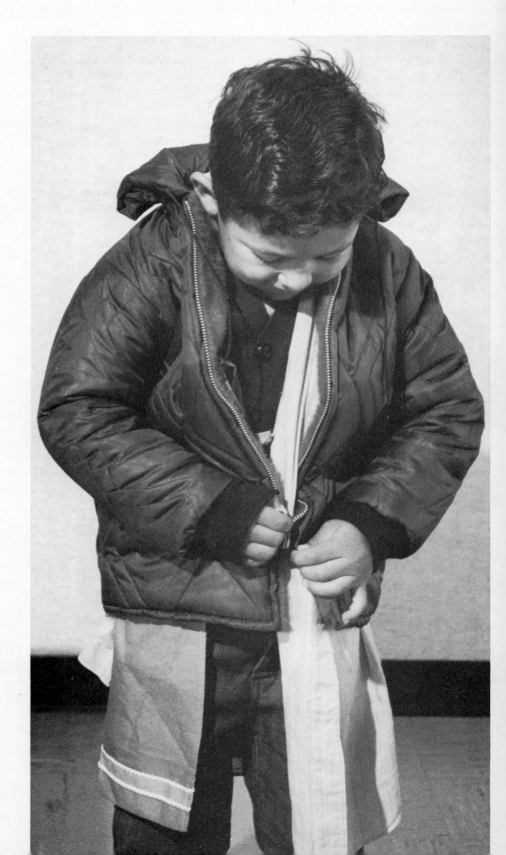

The child selects an article of clothing and puts it on over his regular clothes and fastens it closed. For example, if he chooses the shirt which has hooks and eyes, he hooks the shirt closed. (A large mirror, full length if possible, should be available for the child to use during the process.) Then he puts the next one on over the first, and so on, until all are on. A child who is very confident may like to attempt this task while blindfolded.

The teacher might ask, "Which outfit would you like to put on, David? Put on all the clothes—one on top of the other—and fasten them closed."

Tell me about what you did, David.
What do you call this type of clothing?
How many other shirts/dresses are there in this box?
How many are there altogether? *Counting* this one you have on?
What color is the shirt you have on?
What do you call this pattern?
How does the shirt close? How about this dress?
Do you have anything to wear at home with snaps on it? What? Can you fasten them yourself?
Which piece of clothing do you like best? Least?
What color is the dress with stripes? The shirt with checks?

One pair of shoes large enough that a child can put them over his own shoes and lace them.
Shirts and dresses slightly larger than the child, with various closings including buttons, hooks, snaps, belts, zipper.
Container for the clothes.

Note: It is especially good to have two types of zippers—one a skirt-type zipper and one a jacket-type, which is particularly difficult for young children to learn to zip.

The Bolt Board

Skills Distinguishing among various sizes; learning to think ahead and make predictions; learning how to screw and unscrew a bolt; developing the tactile and visual senses; developing the small muscles used for writing; making comparisons.

The child screws the bolts into the nuts while blindfolded. The task is self-checking since the child must select the correct sizes of nuts and bolts or he will have some left over. Many children will enjoy the challenge of predicting which bolts go with which size nuts *before* they try them. They can place the bolt they think will fit in front of a nut. Sometimes children want to keep a record of how many of these predictions were correct to see if they improve their record on subsequent trials.

Two children often like to work together on this task with blindfolds on. If a tape recording can be obtained, the teacher can gain important insight into children's thinking and language development.

ACTIVITY

The teacher might introduce the activity as follows: "Choose a bolt from this container, Antoinette. Look at the board. Where do you think it will fit? Here? Here? How about here? You try it and see. Put your fingers in the back of the nut and feel what happens as you screw the bolt through. Very good! Find where each bolt goes and then let me see!"

GETTING STARTED

What did you do with all the bolts, Antoinette?

Are *all* the bolts the same size?

Are *any* bolts the same size? Show me.

Show me a bolt that is small. One that is medium sized. One that is large.

Show me a nut that is *not* on the right side of the board. What side is it on? What size is it?

Are there more small nuts and bolts or more large nuts and bolts? Show me.

Point to a bolt that is not medium sized, and not small sized. What size is it? Where is it on the board?

How many nuts and bolts are there altogether? Count them for me, please.

What happens if you try to put the bolt into the nut from the other side? Will it still screw in? Try it and tell me what you find out.

**IDEAS FOR
FOLLOW-UP DISCUSSION**

MATERIALS

One piece of wood 1″ X 1″ X 3′ glued to a 1″ X 4″ X 3′ board.

Five small nuts and bolts.

Five medium nuts and bolts.

Five large nuts and bolts.

Epoxy glue to glue nuts to the small piece of wood.

Container for bolts.

Blindfold.

The Nail Game

Skills Classifying according to size; developing the ability to think ahead and make predictions; developing the tactile and visual senses; making comparisons.

A child takes the can of nails and spreads them out on a small rug so he can see them and so the noise will not disturb other children working. He puts the nails one at a time into the appropriate holes. The task is self-checking: the child ends up with extra nails and the wrong-sized holes if he makes a mistake along the way.

A child who seems to have difficulty with this experience can be given just two sizes of nails to work with at first—the small ones and the very large ones. In this way the child can easily see that there are only two sizes, and prediction will be almost natural.

The teacher might discuss the activity as follows: "See if you can find which hole this nail fits into. Good. What do you think about this one? You're doing fine, Lewis. When all the holes are filled, see if you can see the pattern the nails make."

If a child works for a long time solely by trial and error, the teacher may suggest the following: "Without trying it, Lewis, where do you think that nail might go? Why? Try it and see. Good. How about this nail? What size is it? Are there any nails already in the board that are the same size? Where? Where do you think your nail might go? Why? Try it and see."

Tell me how you put the nails in the board. Did you see any pattern as you were doing it? Was there any way you could tell just by looking at the nail where it was going to go? How?

Show me a small nail. Show me a large nail. Show me a nail in between those sizes. Why is the large sized nail in the wood the same height (just as tall) as the small sized one? How can that be? What makes this one small and this one large? Is it still large when it is *in* the wood? Why?

What shape do the nails outline? What part do the small nails make? What part do the medium ones make? The large?

Piece of wood at least 3-1/2" thick and 8" x 16".
15 small nails (1-1/4") with heads.
15 medium nails (2-1/4") with heads.
15 large nails (3-1/4") with heads.
Hand or power drill with small, medium, and large bits to match the nail sizes.
Container for the nails.

Note: Several pieces of wood may be glued together to attain the needed thickness. Also, because the child will use only his fingers to insert the nails, the holes must be big enough so the nails drop down easily and can be easily lifted out. They should be drilled to whatever depth is necessary so that the heads are all at the same level.

Hook Board

Skills Experiencing one-to-one correspondence; developing hand-eye coordination; strengthening the small muscles used in writing; working with various sizes and distinguishing among them; making comparisons.

The child hangs the washers on the hooks. (A similar hook board may be made with one size hook and the child can form patterns with washers of different sizes and colors.)

ACTIVITY

The teacher might say, "Put one circle on each hook, Lisa." (The child should be left free to discover the possibility of placing the metal washers on the hooks by size.)

GETTING STARTED

What did you do with the metal circles, Lisa?

Tell me about the different sizes you see. Are all the circles the same size? Are *any* of them the same size? Take all the circles off the hooks and put all the same sizes together.

Trace around some of the circles on a piece of paper and try to use the circles as part of your picture. Try it and see how it turns out.

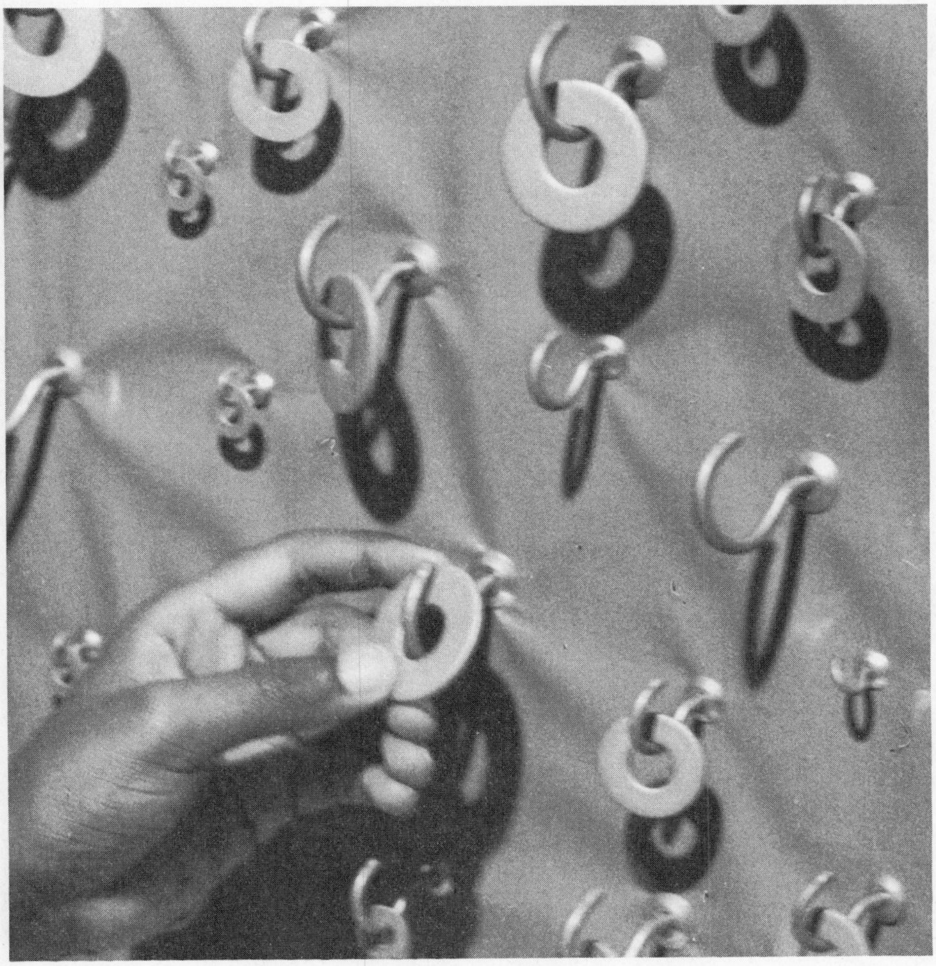

IDEAS FOR
FOLLOW-UP DISCUSSION

Plywood, 12″ x 16″.
Piece of wood nailed to the edge of the plywood to make it stand up.
Spray paint.
Brass cup hooks of various sizes: 10 small, 10 medium, and 10 large.
Metal washers: 10 small, 10 medium, and 10 large.
Container for the metal washers.

MATERIALS

The Pegboards

Skills Observing and reproducing patterns; developing the small muscles; strengthening hand-eye coordination; perceiving differences in color and configuration.

The child reproduces the pattern with colored pegs in the marked-off area of each pegboard.

The difficulty of this workjob is regulated by the difficulty of the pattern. There should be several experiences of each of the types shown below. Three to four pegboards then can be grouped together in one box as a workjob. In this way there may be several different sets of pegboard-pattern workjobs.

The teacher might discuss the activity as follows: "Point to a part of this pattern that is all one color. Good. Now, take some pegs of this color and make the pegboard just like this part of the pattern. Does this look the same as the pattern to you? Are the pegs in the right place? Can you fix it then? Now that's fine. You have the idea now."

What did you do with the pegs, Nathan?

How did you know where to put the pegs and what colors to use?

Tell me about the colors in your pegboard pattern. How many rows, or lines, do you have of red? How many rows of green? Tell me about this part.

Show me a pattern that has two rows of green going across and then two rows of yellow. You tell me about a pattern and I'll guess!

Individual 12″ × 12″ pegboards with a 4″ × 6″ area marked off as the child's working area.

4″ × 6″ tagboard pieces for patterns the child is to repeat.

Colored pencils for coloring the patterns.

Clear contact paper to protect the patterns.

Masking tape to strengthen the edges of the tagboard.

Assorted colored pegs (plastic pegs are far more durable than wooden pegs, and their colors never fade).

Container for pegboards.

Plastic bucket for pegs.

Go-Together Bottles

Skills Associating things that belong together; developing logical thinking; making selections; identifying names of objects.

The child takes the jars with the objects and places them so he can see the objects inside each one. Then he takes the pictures and places them on top of the appropriate jars.

The teacher might ask, "What is inside this jar? Can you find a picture of something that goes with it? Would these two things be used together? How about this? What would be used with it?"

How would these two things be used together? Would *you* ever use them? Would your mother?

Show me something you could use to sew with. Show me something you could write with. Show me something you could burn with.

Show me three things that are black. Show me two things that are red.

Show me something a baby could use. Something you could find in a drawer. Something with legs.

Show me something made of wood. Of plastic. Of metal.

Some children may enjoy matching words to the jars.

20 baby food jars with lids.
Tape to seal the jars closed when objects are inside.
20 objects:

watermelon seeds	pencil eraser	can opener	stamp
tire	key	pill	candles
match	water	hollow egg	buttons
safety pin	flower	pennies	stars
needle	peanuts	fishing hook	nails

20 pictures, backed with cardboard and covered with clear contact paper:

watermelon	pencil	soda can	letter
toy car	door	vitamin bottle	cake
fire	bathtub	hen	shirt
baby's diaper	vase	piggy bank	flag
thread	peanuts in shell	fishing pole	hammer

Container for pictures.
Container for boxed pictures and jars.

The Block Patterns

Skills Perceiving colors and patterns; matching; learning to think ahead; comparing and making judgments; strengthening memory.

A child takes a number of cards and some blocks and builds the pattern beside each model. This workjob is varied by the number of cards a child selects and whether he builds on or off the pattern. A young child may need to build directly on the pattern in the beginning and will benefit from this practice in one-to-one correspondence. As the child gains in skill and confidence he will build by the side of the pattern with ease.

A more mature child may enjoy the challenge of building the pattern from memory by turning the pattern card over before starting to build. More challenging still would be to ask the child to build the mirror image of the pattern. He might begin by placing a mirror on the card at the edge of the pattern and reproducing the reflection *behind* the mirror. As the child gains in skill he will be ready to imagine the reflection, build it, and then check his prediction with the mirror.

GETTING STARTED

The teacher might discuss the activity as follows: "What color blocks are used in this pattern? Take as many blocks as you need and build the pattern beside the answer. Well done. Try the next one."

IDEAS FOR FOLLOW-UP DISCUSSION

What did you do with the blocks?
Do you think you used more than 10 blocks altogether or less than 10? What makes you think so?
What colors did you use in this pattern? This one?
How many red blocks did you need for this pattern? How many green ones? How many blocks altogether did you need?
If I asked you to build this pattern, what color blocks would you need? Show me a pattern that you like. Tell me about it.
If I turn the card over, do you think you could build the pattern again from memory? Try it?

MATERIALS

Tagboard pieces, 6″ × 9″.
1″ construction paper squares in colors to match the cubes.
Rubber cement.
Clear contact paper to cover the answer cards.
1″ cubes of various colors.
Container for cards.
Container for blocks.

Sock Boxes

The child puts his hand into the sock box and feels the item inside. Then he sorts through the pictures to find the one that matches what he feels inside the box and places it on top of the sock box. He repeats this procedure for each box, feeling each item, but never looking at it.

The teacher might discuss the activity as follows: "Put your hand inside and feel what's there. Can you find a picture of what you feel and put it on top of the box?"

What did you find inside the sock boxes? Can you remember without looking at the pictures?
How many boxes are there altogether?
How did this feel? And this?
Show me something that felt soft. Rough. Tickly.
Can you tell me what color this is by feeling? Why not?
Which thing was the nicest one to feel? Why?

*Children who are
ready may label
the objects with words
rather than pictures.*

10 socks.
10 quart-sized plastic containers, approximately 4″ tall, stuffed into the socks.
10 objects to be placed in socks (feather, jacks, pencil, toothbrush, nail, walnuts, toy car, large rubber band, blunt scissors, small ball of yarn).
10 pictures (backed with cardboard and covered with clear contact paper) of the objects placed inside the socks.
Container for sock boxes and boxed pictures.

Note: For ease of checking, a code such as the first three letters of the name of each object can be written on a strip of masking tape and placed on the outside of each box. This enables the teacher to check the pictures without reaching into each sock.

Keys and Locks

Skills Developing hand-eye coordination; strengthening memory; perceiving different sizes and shapes; developing the small muscles; observing an orderly sequence.

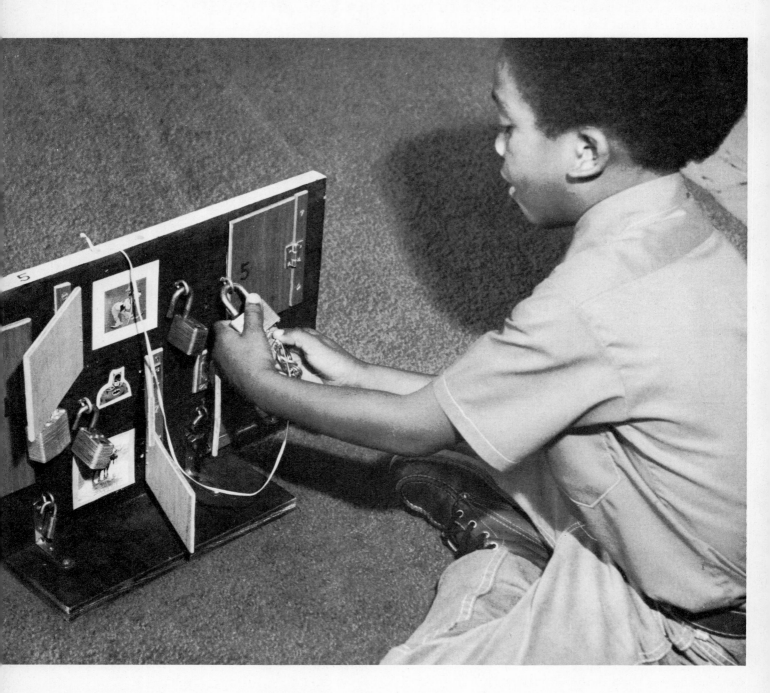

The child unlocks each lock with the appropriate key. When he is finished, he locks each lock and hangs up the keys.

The teacher might say, "See if you can open all the locks!"

Tell me how you did your workjob, Mark.
What are these called? And these?
How many locks are there all together?
Are there more locks than keys?
If I took away this key, would you be able to open *all* the locks?
Do you need the keys to put the locks back on and close them? Try and find out.
Do you have any locks like these at home?
What locks have you been allowed to open at home?
Do we have any locks in our classroom? See if you can find out how many.

A piece of plywood approximately 1' x 18".
Small doors hinged to a strip of wood to be nailed to the plywood.
Rings or fasteners on which to hang the locks.
Assorted locks and keys.
Key chain for keys.
A piece of wood approximately 1' x 4" x 6" to nail to the edge of the plywood to make it stand up.
Hook on which the keys may be hung.
Funny pictures to be glued inside each door.

Note: The difficulty of this workjob depends on the number of locks included. A combination lock can provide a great challenge.

The Screw Game

Skills Observing size differences; making predictions; developing the small muscles used in writing; learning to use a screwdriver to put in and remove screws.

The child screws each metal screw into the correctly sized nut on the board with his screwdriver.

This workjob is especially well suited to the boys in the classroom, and they often like to pair up and do it together. The resulting conversation often is well worth recording on tape. The boys in class also seem to especially enjoy using a stopwatch with this activity to time the process of screwing in each bolt. Some of them time the whole process and compete with one another for the best time. Others work together and time how long it takes to screw in one bolt and then try to increase their speed with each succeeding bolt. Some children even like to count the number of turns it takes different sized screws to go into the board.

The teacher might ask, "Can you screw these screws into the holes, Charles?"

GETTING STARTED

What have you been working with, Charles?
Tell me what you did.
What are these called?
How did you go about putting the screws into the wood?
Are all the screws the same size, Charles? Tell me about the sizes.
Have you ever used a screwdriver at home? What for?
Did you ever see someone else using a screwdriver? What for? Who?

**IDEAS FOR
FOLLOW-UP DISCUSSION**

MATERIALS

One piece of wood at least 1-1/2" thick.
A drill for drilling holes into the wood.
Epoxy glue to glue the nuts over the holes in the wood.
15 stove bolts with matching nuts.
A short-handled (4") screwdriver (much easier for a young child to manipulate than a long-handled one).
Container for screws and screwdriver.

Note: The nuts can be hammered flush with the wood so they will stay firmly in place.

Matching

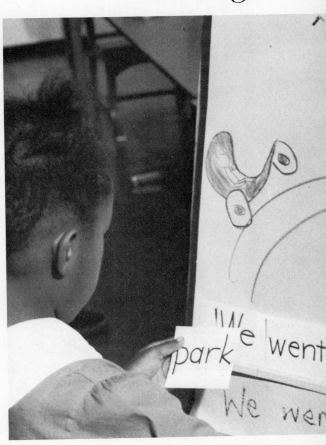

The Outline Game

Skills One-to-one correspondence; observing the shapes of objects; noticing similarities and differences; matching.

The child takes the objects out of the box one at a time and names the item. He then tries to place the object on its outline in only one trial.

Children who are very confident may like the challenge of attempting to reproduce the arrangement *off* the answerboard.

The teacher might discuss the activity as follows: "Can you find what shape this flag is on the answerboard? Why do you choose this one? Good thinking! Try it and see. Does it fit? Good. Find where all the objects go."

What did you do with the objects, Christopher?

How did you know where they would go on the answerboard?

Point to an object that is round. Point to one that is made of rubber.

How many objects are green? How many are *not* white, *not* red, or *not* brown? Show me.

What kind of material is this block made of? This bobby pin?

Show me something used to hold things together.

Show me something that cuts.

Point to an object that unlocks a lock.

Would you like to make a book of shapes? Find an object and trace around it on this paper. Bring it to me and I'll write the word for the object for you. When you have five pages, we'll put them together in a book.

Two 12″ x 18″ pieces of tagboard and cardboard.

Colored pencils to color outlines.

Clear contact paper to protect answerboard.

Masking tape to strengthen all edges.

Cloth tape for making hinges between the two sections of answerboard.

Small objects: block, key, chain, book, scissors, buttons, bobby pin, colored rubber bands, toys, paper clips, rings, comb, clothespin, flag, corks, etc.

Container for objects.

The Little Rugs

Skills Distinguishing similarities and differences in color, texture, and pattern; developing the tactile and visual senses; making comparisons.

A child scatters the squares backed with tagboard on the floor. He takes
a loose material square and looks for the matching square on the floor.
He then places the matching square on top of the square on the floor.

When he is finished, the child places all the tagboard-backed squares
in one box and the loose material squares in the second box. This
automatically shuffles the pieces for the next child's use.

After completing this activity, the child may enjoy working with the
squares in another way. He might choose any specific number of
squares and take them outside the classroom to the cement where he
can chalk out the area he thinks his squares would cover. Then he can
lay the squares down and check his estimation. Children become
increasingly accurate in their estimations with more frequent trials and
are often very impressed with this new found power.

The teacher might say, "Scatter the squares with paper on the back
around on the floor. Then see if you can find the material on the floor
that matches these other squares."

What have you been doing? How did you go about it? Show me.
Gather up all the squares with plaid material and give them to me. And
    all the ones with stripes.
Point to all the squares that have red in them. Show me the squares that
    have yellow or white in them. Give me a square that does not have
    orange, or green, or red in it.
How many squares are there that are solid colors? Count them for me
    please.
Do you have a favorite pattern?
Show me some material that reminds you of something you have at
    home. Is there any material like the material on your couch or on a
    chair?

Two (4″ x 4″) squares of 25 different materials (to form 25 pairs).
6″ x 6″ tagboard to back one square of each pair.
Glue.
Box for tagboard-backed squares.
Box for loose material squares.
Large box for the two individual boxes.

Note: Any large upholstery store will gladly give a teacher its old sample books.
Upholstery is excellent for this workjob because it is strong, does not unravel easily,
and comes in 4″ x 8″ pieces.

The Part-Whole Game

Skills Learning to look for clues; paying attention to details; seeing the relationship of part to whole; matching.

The child places the picture pieces in the appropriate place on the answerboard, matching the parts with the correct picture. A child who has difficulty with this activity can be given the pictures of the "parts" drawn on clear acetate. In this case, he can place the "part" directly on the "whole" and see that it matches. When the child becomes more sure of himself, he can assemble the parts off the answerboard without having to try them first on the picture.

The teacher may want to make several different sets of part-whole games so the children can have a wide variety of experiences through which to increase their skill.

The teacher might discuss the activity as follows: "Look carefully at this paper, Vincent. Can you find this same part on the answerboard? What makes you say this part is the same? I agree! How about these other pieces? Where do they go?"

Tell me about all these little pieces of paper, Vincent.
How do you know this part goes here?
Can you tell about the whole picture from looking at these small pieces? Why not?
What is this a picture of? And this?
How many pieces are part of the first picture? How many are part of the third?
Which picture has the most parts matched with it?

12″ x 18″ tagboard and cardboard.
Three photographs or pictures cut from magazines.
Clear contact paper to protect pictures.
Masking tape to strengthen edges.
Three to five pieces cut from pictures identical to those on the answerboard.
Container for cards.

The Letter Boxes

Skills Recognizing similarities and differences; observing letter form; matching; making comparisons.

The child sorts the letter cards into the boxes with the matching letters. Similar workjobs can be made to help the child advance through various stages of reading readiness.

A first game might be made with a color on each box and matching colors on a set of cards to be sorted by the child into the boxes. A variation might be different shades of the color placed on the cards to be sorted into the boxes.

Another game could use different geometric shapes to be sorted. A more difficult set could employ two or three shapes together on each box.

The final game in the series might be several letters placed on each box such as

fan fat rat tan fun rot

In this way the child is gaining important perceptual training in observing letter sequence which is essential in word discrimination in reading.

The teacher, comparing the letter card with each letter on the front of the boxes, might ask, "Is this letter the same, Sherry? Where can it go?"

GETTING STARTED

What did you do with the cards, Sherry?

Point to a sound you know. Good. Do you know any others? Show me the one that sounds like "mmmm."

How are these two letters different? Are they the same in any way?

Which letters have a circle as part of them? A straight line which goes above the line? A curved line that goes below the line?

Are any of these letters in your name?

**IDEAS FOR
FOLLOW-UP DISCUSSION**

MATERIALS

Empty 1/2-pint milk cartons, tops removed.
Paper to cover cartons.
Clear contact paper to protect covered cartons.
Marking pen to write letters.
Tagboard strips, 1-1/2″ × 6″ (five to ten for each letter in the series).
Container for cards.
Container for letter boxes and boxed cards.

Matching 57

Labeling

Children should be very familiar with the labels around the classroom before beginning this workjob. The child selects some cards with words written on them. He matches them one at a time with real objects labeled in the classroom. He draws a picture of each object. Then he practices writing the word with a transparency over it and, when he is ready, writes it under his picture. Two children may enjoy working together on this activity.

The teacher might discuss the activity as follows: "Choose some word cards, Suzanne. See if you can find out what the words say by matching them to the words around the classroom. Draw a picture for each of your words and try to write the word when you finish."

What do your words say, Suzanne? How did you find out?
What is the sound this word begins with?
Which word starts with "b"?
Point to the word that names what we use to enter and leave our classroom. How many doors are there in this room? Show me.
Which word names what we look out of to see the outside while we're still inside?
How many words can you read?

2″ x 6″ cards (two for each label).
Marking pen to write words for objects in the classroom (door, piano, wall, window, clock, books, table, chair, ceiling, etc.).
3″ x 7″ piece of cardboard and transparency taped on three sides with masking tape, making an envelope.
Crayon.
Tissue or cloth.
Paper for making a book.
Container for cards and plastic envelopes.

Note: One label is affixed to the object it names in the classroom. The other label is kept with the workjob.

Individual Sentence Charts

Skills Experiencing the ability to draw and write about what one thinks and share it with other people; matching words in a sentence; reading; writing practice.

The child draws or paints a picture. The teacher then writes at the bottom what the child tells about his picture. The child may try to write under the teacher's words. Later, the teacher writes the words from the sentence and puts on the tag strip to form pockets. The child then can match the individual words to the words in his sentence and practice reading.

Children can make books of these individual sentence pictures. When they have three or more sentences, they can mix up all the words from the sentences and learn the words individually as well as match them.

When the child has finished painting, the teacher might say, "Tell me about your painting. What would you like me to write down about your picture? Good. Read it to me. Would you like to try writing under my writing?" When the child is ready to match the word cards to the words in the sentence, the teacher can say, "Find where these words go in your sentence."

Tell me about your work. What is this at the bottom? Read it to me please.
Which word says "park"? Which one says "car"?
How many words are in your sentence?
Is this sentence you wrote today longer or shorter than the last one you wrote? Show me.
How many letters are in this word?
What do we call this area between the words? What is it for?
What is this mark at the end of the sentence called?
Which is your favorite picture of all the ones you've done? Why?
Mix up all the words from these three sentences, and see how many you can read to me.

Easel paper.
Paints and brushes for the child to paint pictures.
Marking pen for the teacher to write the child's sentence as it is dictated.
1" strip of tagboard taped to the bottom of each picture, making a pocket chart.
Word cards for writing each word of the child's sentence.

Spelling

The child matches the linking letters to the letters under the pictures and spells out words. When a child shows real confidence in this game he can cover the word traced on the picture with a strip of construction paper, scramble the letters in the word, and try to spell the word. He can remove the paper strip and check his work.

Eventually the child will be able to scramble the letters from all the words and reassemble them without having to look at the spelling.

The teacher will want to have a series of similar games using different words to give the children more experience.

The teacher might discuss the activity as follows: "What's this a picture of, Alicia? Do you have one? Would you like one? What do you think this word is? Very smart of you! To make this word, you need to find each letter and put them together. Can you find this letter under the picture of the airplane? Good! And what letter are you going to look for next?"

How many letters are in this word?
What do you think this word says? And this one?
How does this word start—with what sound?
Which word starts with the sound "ffff"? With "mmmmmm"?

Pictures cut from magazines or drawn by children.
9" x 12" tagboard to back each picture.
Rubber cement.
Clear contact paper to protect the pictures.
Linking letters needed to spell words.
Container for linking letters.
Container for cards and boxed letters.

Note: It is helpful to trace around the linking shape with a pencil and write the letters in each shape *before* using the clear contact paper.

The Mailman

Skills Observing numerals in a series; matching; role-playing; noticing small details; strengthening left-to-right progression.

The child takes the folder of houses and envelopes and places the houses so he can see each house number. He matches each envelope to the house with the same number, so as to "deliver the mail."

A child who shows an interest in doing this workjob but finds it too difficult may work with three to five houses and envelopes and work gradually up to ten.

The teacher might discuss the activity as follows: "Moses, have you ever gotten a letter at your house? How did the mailman know to deliver it to your house instead of the house next door? Look at this house and these two envelopes. Is there anything that is the same about this house and one of these envelopes?"

How did you go about delivering the mail, Moses?
But how did you know that this letter should go to this house? Why didn't it go next door?
What is this writing on a letter called? And what is this called? Why do we put stamps on a letter?
What is this house number? What is your house number at home? What is the city you live in? Are all the letters you delivered in the same city? Are they all on the same street?
How many houses are there? How many envelopes? Were there more envelopes than houses?
Point to all the houses that have the numeral 6 in their house number. Are there any house numbers that do *not* have the numeral 1?

Tagboard on which the children have drawn pictures of their houses.
Scissors for cutting out the houses.
Marking pen for writing house numbers.
Envelopes and stamps.
Names and addresses of the children in class whose houses are used.
Paper mailman's hat and mail pouch.
Container for mail pouch, hat, letters, and houses.

Classification

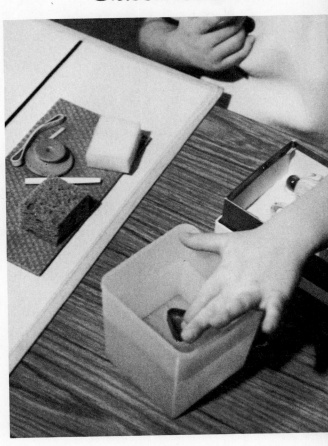

The Food Game

The child sorts the empty packages onto the appropriate fruit card.

The teacher might discuss the activity as follows: "What is the name of this fruit? And this one? And this one? Take one of the boxes here and look at it carefully. Can you tell what flavor of fruit was used? Good. Where do you think the applesauce should go?"

Tell me about all the things with apples in them.
Tell me about the things with cherries in them.
Show me a fruit that is orange and is sweet. Show me another fruit that is sweet. What do we call this? Show me a fruit that is *not* sweet. What is it called? How does it taste? Show me a fruit that looks just like this fruit in shape but it is a different color.
Show me a fruit that grows in Africa. One that grows in California. One that grows in Hawaii.
Name all the fruits that are yellow.
Show me a fruit that comes in a bunch. Another one.
What fruit is spelled "b-a-n-a-n-a"?

10" x 16" pieces of tagboard.
Pictures of fruits.
Glue.
Clear contact paper to protect tagboard and containers.
Marking pen to write names of fruits.
Plastic fruits to match pictures.
Empty food packages that contained fruit or fruit products.
  Apples: applesauce, apple strudel, apple pie, apple juice, baked apples, Applette candy bar
  Pears: pear nectar, canned pears
  Grapes: wine, grape juice, raisins, grape jelly, grape chewing gum
  Oranges: orange juice, orange marmalade, orange Jello, orange cake mix
  Bananas: banana cream pie, banana cake, banana muffins, banana nut bread
  Cherries: cherry Jello, cherry cookies, maraschino cherries, cherry cough drops, cherry pie
  Pineapples: canned pineapple slices, pineapple juice, pineapple upside-down cake
  Strawberries: strawberry jelly, frozen berries, strawberry Jello, strawberry cheese cake, strawberry yogurt
  Lemons: lemonade, lemon juice, lemon cookies, lemon cake
  Peaches: peach pie, peach jam, canned peaches, peach nectar
Container for cards.
Large container for empty boxes and boxed cards.

Patterns

The child sorts the patterns he sees into the sorting box according to ACTIVITY whether they are striped, plain-colored, polka dotted, print, plaid, or checked.

Children should know the vocabulary involved before they work with this activity. The teacher might make a chart of the possible patterns and have the children tell about their clothing patterns the week before this activity is presented.

Some children may enjoy a related follow-up activity of surveying the class to see how many children are wearing each of these patterns. The teacher might prepare a strip of tagboard similar to the one on the sorting box that has a picture of the possible patterns. The child can tape this so it hangs over the edge of a table and then place a block for each child in the classroom wearing plaid clothing above the plaid pattern, a block for each child in the room wearing plain-colored clothing, and so forth until all the possibilities are covered. Sometimes a child will want to use one color block for boy's patterns and another for girls. Other children may prefer to make a separate graph for the boys and one for the girls. Still other children like to have each person write his name on a strip of masking tape to stick to a block. Regardless of the way of recording the findings, children gain much understanding from this experience of comparing.

The teacher might discuss the activity as follows: "What pattern is this? **GETTING STARTED** Is it a plain color? Is it striped? Is it print? Okay, can you show me where this would go in the sorting box? Yes! Good for you. How about this one?"

As I point to these patterns, please tell me what they are called. **IDEAS FOR**
FOLLOW-UP DISCUSSION
What pattern is your shirt? Your slacks? Your socks? My dress? Valerie's skirt?
Show me someone in the classroom who is wearing something plaid. Someone who has on a plain color. What color is it?
How many polka dot patterns did you have to sort? How many checks? Which is your favorite pattern? What color is it?

Pictures of clothes cut from catalogs and magazines showing various patterns in **MATERIALS** materials.
Rubber cement.
Tagboard pieces 4" x 6" on which pictures are pasted.
Clear contact paper to protect pictures.
Sorting box made from cardboard, with slots taped to the top and bottom.
Paint to paint sorting box.
Pictures of patterns pasted above each slot.
Container for pattern cards.

Animal Habitat

Skills Learning about the natural environment of various animals; classifying animals according to their habitat; making comparisons; drawing conclusions.

The child sorts the pictures under the appropriate categories, placing together the animals which live mostly in the water, those which live mostly on land, and those which live mostly in the air.

Teachers may want to have several sets of pictures for the children to sort with this answerboard. They might select pictures of vehicles or machinery such as a submarine for "in water," a lawn mower for "on land," and an airplane for "in the air." Another group of pictures could be prepared for uniforms that might be worn in these categories such as a deep-sea diver's outfit for "in water," a football uniform for "on land," and an astronaut's suit for "in the air."

The teacher might discuss the activity as follows: "If an animal lives mostly on the land, where will his picture go? If he lives mostly in the air, where will his picture go? If he lives mostly in the water, where will his picture go? Put the pictures where you think the animals live most of the time."

Name all the animals that live mostly in the water. Those that live mostly in the air, and those that live mostly on the land.
Name an animal that is very small and lives on the land. Name one that is huge.
Do you know the name of the largest bird? The largest animal? The tallest one?
Put all the animals with horns in one pile.
Show me some animals whose names you do not know, and I'll tell you their names.

9" X 12" sheets of tagboard, cardboard, and clear contact paper.
Marking pen for drawing habitats.
Cotton for clouds.
Cloth tape for hinging sections of answerboard together.
Pictures of animals that live mostly in the water, mostly on land, and mostly in the air.
Clear contact paper to protect pictures.
Container for pictures and folded answerboard.

Days of the Week

Skills Learning the days of the week; reading; learning about the calendar; reinforcing left-to-right progression.

The child places the cards in order, with Sunday first, then Monday, and so forth, to show the days of the week.

Each child should have a calendar for reference as he orders the days of the week. If it is across the room, so much the better, for the child will be strengthening his memory by keeping the word pattern in his mind as he walks back to where he is working.

The teacher might like to make similar games for the months of the year or for ordinal sequence, listing first, second, third, and so forth.

The teacher might discuss the activity as follows: "What is the first day of the week? It's the day some people go to church. Yes, Sunday. And which day comes next? Good. Can you put the days after this in order?"

Which day is the first school day of the week? What is the first day of the week?

Which is the last day of the week? What do you do on this day?

How many days are there in a week? How many of these days do you go to school? How many are in the weekend?

Which day of the week begins with a "W"? With an "M"?

On which day do we go to the library? On which day do we do creative dramatics?

Look at the menu for the cafeteria and find out for me which day we are going to have hot dogs. When you have found out, I'll write the word on this paper for you, and you can draw the hot dogs!

Paper for cutting out the outlines of seven train cars.

Black marking pen for writing the days of the week on the cars.

Clear contact paper to protect the train cars.

Pictures of class activities done on particular days to be sorted with the appropriate train car.

Container for the train.

The Word Board

Skills Reading; matching; strengthening visual memory; classifying; distinguishing word forms; generalizing.

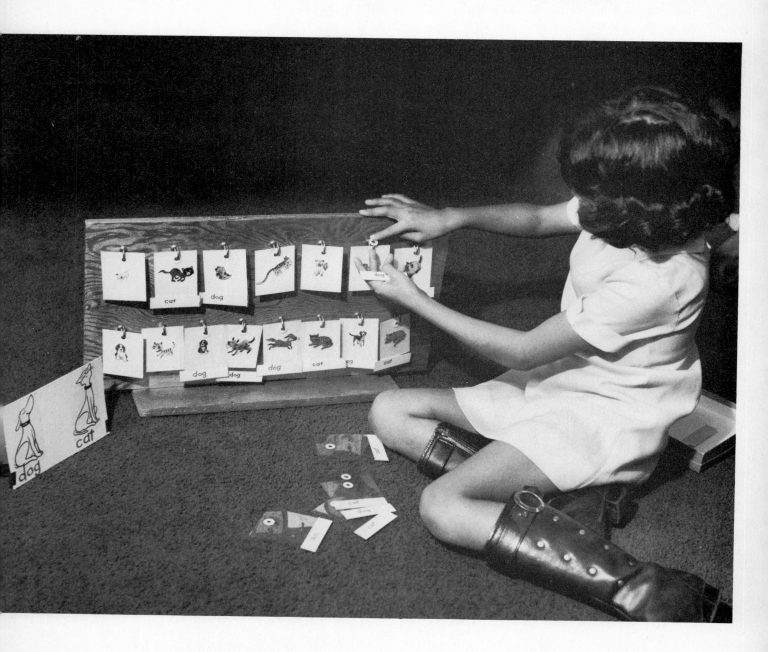

The child hangs up the pictures on the answerboard and matches the words to the appropriate pictures.

The teacher might point to the reference card and ask, "What do you think these words say?" Then, looking to the answerboard, "What do you think this word might be? What can you do with the label?"

Tell me about your work, Noemi.
Spell "dog" without peeking. Spell "cat."
How many pictures of dogs are there? How many pictures of cats are there? Which are there more of?
What is the first sound in "cat"? What is the last sound in "dog"?
Would you like to write these words on the board? Good. When you finish, find a friend and see if he can read your words.

1' x 2' board.
6" x 2' rectangle of wood nailed to the edge of the board to make it stand up.
15 hooks screwed at even intervals into the answerboard.
Spray paint.
2" x 3" pieces of tagboard.
Pictures in two categories.
Rubber cement.
Clear contact paper to protect pictures.
Hole punch.
2" x 3" pieces of transparency.
Marking pen to write category on transparency.
6" x 9" piece of tagboard.
Pictures of categories.
Marking pen for writing label.
Clear contact paper.
Container for cards and reference sheet.

Float and Sink

Skills Developing the ability to categorize; developing the tactile-visual sense; making judgments; experiencing the properties of water; learning that some things float in water and others sink; developing the concept of opposites.

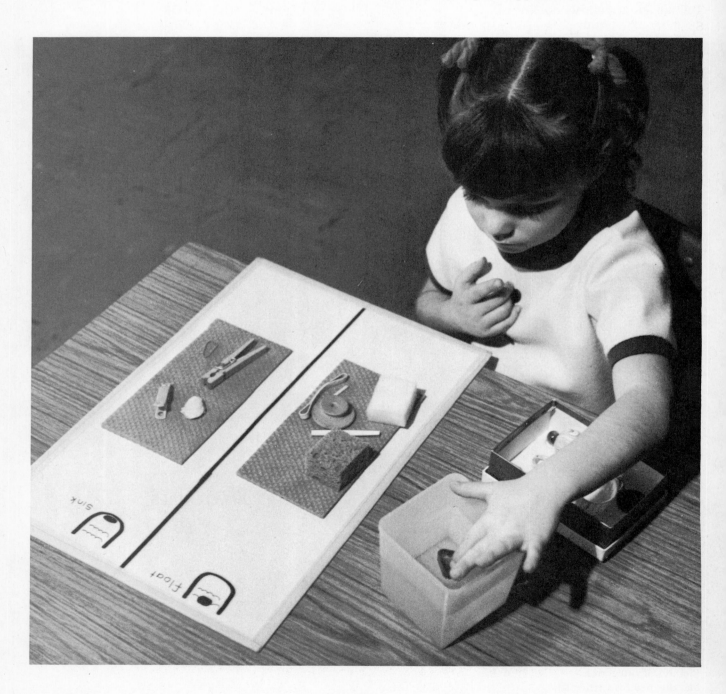

The child fills the water container and, through trial and error, determines whether each object sinks or floats when placed in water. The object is placed on the appropriate side of the answerboard. A mature child may enjoy recording his predictions and his findings.

Children love follow-up activities to the sink and float game where they concentrate on observing the water level when objects are lowered into the container. They mark the original water level on the jar with crayon. Then they try different sized rocks but first estimate by sliding a rubber band around the jar to the level they predict the water will rise to. Then they place the rock in the water and check how close their estimation was. The more experience they have, the more accurate their predictions become!

The teacher might point to the answerboard and say, "This picture shows a container of water like yours. Point to the picture where the object in the water is at the top. Does this object float or sink? Show me the picture where the object is at the bottom. Does it float or does it sink in the water? Good. Now, if you try this object in water and it floats, where will you put it on the answerboard? Why?"

What have you been working with, Gina?

What does this word say? And this one?

Explain the picture on the left side of the answerboard. Why is the picture there? What's it for?

How many objects did you find that would float?

What are these objects made of?

Show me an object that floats. Can you make it sink some way? Try it and see, and then come and get me.

Did more things float or more sink? When you find out, tell me by writing it on the board.

12″ x 18″ tagboard sheet.
Cardboard to back the tagboard.
Clear contact paper for front and back to prevent cardboard from getting wet and warping.
Masking tape to strengthen all edges.
Felt pens.
Assorted objects for experimenting. If possible, some should look identical, but one should float while the other, although similar, sinks—for example, Ivory and Camay guest soaps, and equal pieces of ebony and pine woods.
Container for water.
Thin sponge to catch the water from the objects (to be placed on the answerboard).
Container for objects (lined with contact paper to make it leak proof).

Classification 79

Rough and Smooth

Skills Concentrating on an awareness of the tactile sense; categorizing by texture; making comparisons.

The child looks at each card to determine whether the object pictured is rough or smooth, and then places it on the appropriate side of the answerboard.

A child who has difficulty with this activity should sort real objects first into rough and smooth piles. He might even try this blindfolded.

A child who can read several words might enjoy the challenge of the task of sorting words into these categories. For example, "brick" would be rough and "spoon" would be smooth.

Children also enjoy cutting pictures from magazines and writing the category by each picture.

Looking at the answerboard, the teacher might say, "Point to a word on the answerboard, Ronald. It says 'rough'. How does rough feel? Yes. I might have written 'bumpy.' 'Rough' is another way of saying 'bumpy.' This other word is 'smooth.' How would a real watermelon feel? On which side of the answerboard do you think it should go? Why?"

Tell me how you divided the cards, Ronald.
Why are all these things together? Why did you put them on this side of the answerboard instead of over here?
Tell me how this would feel. Tell me why you put this here.

12″ x 18″ tagboard.
Cardboard to back tagboard.
Marking pen.
Clear contact paper to cover answerboard.
Masking tape to strengthen all edges.
Assorted pictures of objects of rough and smooth texture.
Tagboard to back pictures.
Glue.
Container for pictures.

Note: When working with very young children it is helpful to place a 3″ square of satin on the smooth side and a 3″ square of sandpaper on the rough side of the answerboard.

The Same-Difference Game

Skills Seeing similarities and differences; noticing details; making comparisons of symbols and pictures; developing a concept of opposites.

The child sorts through the cards one at a time and decides whether the pictures are the "same" or "different." If they are the same, they are placed on the right side (over the two pieces of paper that are the same color); if they are different, they are placed on the left (over the two pieces of paper that are different from one another).

ACTIVITY

Looking at the answerboard, the teacher might say, "Show me the side where the two pieces of construction paper are the *same* color. Good. Now, what do you think this word might be? Good! Now, point to the side where the two pieces of paper are different. What do you think this word might be? Now, if you have a card like this where both pictures are the same, where would you put it on the answerboard? Why?"

GETTING STARTED

Tell me what you've been doing, James.
Why did you put all these cards together in the same pile? And why did you choose this side of the answerboard to put them on?
Would it be okay with you if I put this card over on this other side instead of here? Why not?
Where are the pictures that are different? Tell me what is different about these two pictures. And these.
What is this a picture of?
What color is this dress? And this house? And this ball?

IDEAS FOR FOLLOW-UP DISCUSSION

MATERIALS

12″ x 18″ tagboard.
Cardboard to back the tagboard.
Four 4″ x 9″ pieces of construction paper.
Marking pen to line one of the pieces of construction paper.
Clear contact paper to protect the answerboard.
Masking tape to strengthen all edges.
Pictures, handmade or commercially prepared (from dittos, workbooks, charts, etc.) showing similarities and differences.
Cardboard to back the pictures.
Clear contact paper to cover the pictures.

People Pictures

Skills Becoming aware of various feelings; classifying; developing the ability to form judgments; seeing similarities and differences.

A child takes the pictures and sorts them in some way.

Some children will sort in the obvious way—happy and sad. Other children separate all the men, all the women, and all the men and women who are happy or sad. Still others have elaborate schemes for sorting such as *why* the people might feel as they do. If free to do so, most children will think of their own categories.

The teacher might discuss the activity as follows: "Christopher, look at these pictures and tell me about them. Do you remember when you sorted the buttons and the fish and the nuts? How could you sort these pictures into two groups? Are there any pictures that have something the same about them that you could put into one group?"

Tell me about these people, Christopher.

Why did you put all these pictures together here? And these?

How do you think this person feels? What can you think of that might have caused him to feel this way?

Is there a picture that reminds you of some way you once felt? Why?

How might I look if I had just burned my dinner in the oven? Is there a picture that shows someone looking like that?

Is there a picture that would show how you might look if you had just had your new bike stolen?

How about a picture of how someone might look if he had been offered a big piece of cake? Do you like cake? How might you look if you didn't like cake?

Would you like to make a book? Can you find pictures of happy people and sad people (or men and women, or children and grownups, or fat people and skinny people, or whatever the child has been working with) in this magazine?

Pictures cut from magazines, mounted on tagboard, showing a variety of emotions.
Clear contact paper for protecting pictures.
Container for pictures.

The Language Boxes

Skills Following directions; learning the meaning of various prepositional phrases.

The child puts out the boxes and places the cubes according to the teacher's directions. The teacher places one cube under a box, one on top of another, one in a corner, etc., and asks the child to tell her where each cube is as she indicates the boxes. If the child has difficulty with any of them, he is asked to involve himself, as by crawling *under* the table, sitting *on top* of the desk, and so on.

Children may enjoy working together, one placing the cube and the other telling where it has been placed.

The teacher might direct the child's work in one of the following ways:
"Stand on top of the table! Now, put one cube *on top* of each box."
"Where am I standing? Put the cubes *beside* the boxes."
"Go stand in a corner of the classroom. And now put the cubes in the *corner* of each box."
"I'm going to do something with this cube and this box." (The teacher moves the box away from the others.) "Turn around!" (Teacher puts the cube under the box.) "You can look now. What did I do with the cube? Yes! You do it with the other cubes."
"This time I want you to put the cube *inside* the boxes."
"Stand *between* me and the chalkboard. Good. Can you guess where I want you to put the cubes this time?"

Where is the cube?
If I put the cube on top of the box, where is the box?
Is this cube between the boxes or behind the boxes?

10 small boxes.
10 small cubes.
Container for cubes.
Container for boxed cubes and boxes.

Weight Boxes

The child sorts through the weight boxes to find the pairs of identical weight. He puts each pair on a separate answerboard.

A child who has great difficulty might use a simple balance to weigh his pairs, while one who does this workjob easily may be asked to put his pairs in order according to graduated weight.

The teacher might say, "See if you can find the pairs that are the same weight and put them together."

What have you been doing?
Which pair of weights is the heaviest? Which is the lightest?
Would a lemon be heavier or lighter than this weight?
Can you find something in the classroom that is about the same weight as this one?
Pick up two weights and show me the heavier one.

Tagboard squares.
Felt marking pen.
Containers of equal size to be filled at different levels with plaster of paris.
Spray paint to hide the plaster level.
Container for cards and weights.

Note: The difference in the amount of plaster in the pairs should be great enough to be easily detected. One pair can be empty. The next can have 1/4 cup plaster mixed with water. The next can have 3/4 cup plaster, and the next 1-1/4 cup, etc.

Sniffing Bottles

Skills Developing olfactory perception; making selections from smells; matching pictures of objects with that object's smell.

The child opens each jar *one at a time* and sniffs. (If several jars are opened at once and the tops mixed up, the scents are not as distinct.) The child places the picture of what he thinks is inside each jar on top.

ACTIVITY

The teacher might say, "Open a jar and smell what's inside. See if you can find the picture that goes with that smell. Try the others."

GETTING STARTED

Let me smell the jar with something inside it that grownups mix with water to make a hot drink.
Show me something you might smell on a picnic.
Show me what men splash on their faces after shaving off their whiskers.

IDEAS FOR
FOLLOW-UP DISCUSSION

10 baby food jars with lids.
10 squares of gauze to wrap smelly items in.
Smelly items:

peppermint	after shave lotion
peanut butter	pickle
wedge of lemon (replace once a week)	cinnamon stick
cocoa	cloves or peppercorns
ground coffee	Vicks VapoRub

A picture of each item, backed with cardboard and covered with clear contact paper.
Spray paint to make the jars opaque.
Container for cards.
Container for jars and boxed cards.

MATERIALS

Note: The teacher can write a code, such as the first three letters of the smell, on a strip of masking tape and place it on the outside of each jar. This permits a quick check of the child's work without having to smell each jar.

Hard-Soft

ACTIVITY

The child takes the cards and sorts them into the two piles on the answerboard. If the picture is of something which is soft, it is placed on the right side of the answerboard, which says "soft." If it is hard, it is placed on the left side.

Children who have any difficulty with this task should sort real objects first into hard and soft. When a child can read the words involved he could sort words such as "cat" for soft and "rock" for hard, and so forth.

GETTING STARTED

The teacher might discuss the activity as follows: "If this picture were the real thing—a real hammer—would it feel hard or soft? Which side of the answerboard has the word "hard" on it? Is the wood hard or soft? That's your clue, isn't it? Where will the picture of the hammer go then? What about the next picture?"

IDEAS FOR FOLLOW-UP DISCUSSION

What did you do with the pile of pictures? How did you decide which side of the answerboard they would go on?
What is the name of each of these pictures?
Is there anything that you don't know the name of?
Spell the word "hard." Spell the word "soft."
(Looking at an item incorrectly placed) If you were to hold one of these—a real one—would it feel hard or soft?
Which one of these things would you like best to feel? Why?
What are you wearing that is hard? What is soft?

MATERIALS

9" X 12" tagboard, cardboard, and clear contact paper.
Masking tape to strengthen all edges.
Piece of wood and marking pen to write "hard."
Piece of sponge and marking pen to write "soft."
Pictures of hard/soft objects, backed with cardboard and covered with clear contact paper.

Hard

hammer	soap	bone
chest	mirror	seashell
chair	cup	marbles
money	turtle	telephone

Soft

shirt	feather	slippers
grapes	teddy bear	towels
bread	chicken	yarn
sweater	kitten	snowman

Container for pictures.

Work-Play

The child sorts the pictures into two piles on the answerboard according to whether work or play is pictured.

ACTIVITY

The teacher might discuss the activity as follows: "Take one of the cards and tell me what the person is doing. Is he working or playing? Which side of the answerboard would you put it on then? Why? That's good thinking! Now, how about the next card?

GETTING STARTED

What did you do with the pictures? How did you decide where you would put them on the answerboard?

IDEAS FOR
FOLLOW-UP DISCUSSION

What is each person doing in this pile of pictures?
Where is the word "work"? Where is the word "play"? How do you spell them?
What does your mother do most—work or play? What do you do most? What does your dog do most?
What kind of work do you think is fun? What kind of play?
What is hard to do when you are playing? What is the hardest work you can think of?
Would you like to write one of these words on the board?

9″ x 12″ tagboard, cardboard, and clear contact paper.
Pictures of someone working and someone playing.
Marking pen to write "work" and "play."
Masking tape to strengthen all edges.
Pictures of people working and playing, backed with cardboard and covered with clear contact paper.
Container for pictures.

MATERIALS

The Feely Board

Skills Developing tactile perception; making selections using only the sense of touch; feeling similarities and differences; describing textures; matching.

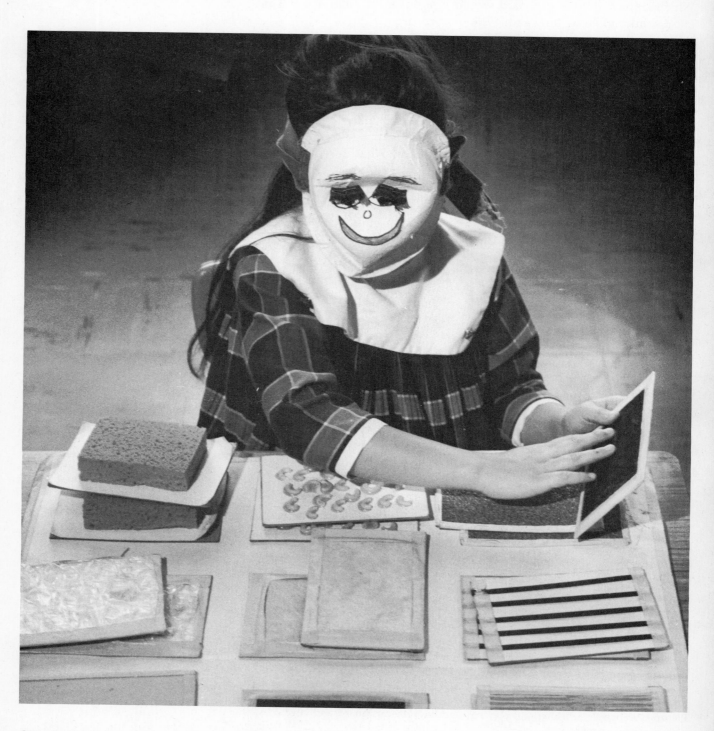

Wearing a blindfold, the child matches each card to its mate on the answerboard by feeling the textures.

The teacher might say, "I'll tie the blindfold on you. Now, see if you can find the pair that matches this card on the answerboard."

Tell me how some of these things feel.
Show me something bumpy. Something smooth. Something that stretches.
Can you tell by *smelling* this material how it will feel? How about if you *look* at it?
How many things feel good to you? Is there anything you don't like to feel? Why?
Where is the thing blind people read? Do they read it with their eyes? Why not? What do they use?
Would this feel any differently if you felt it with your feet instead of your fingers? Try it and see. Would you like to work with a partner and do the game again, feeling with your feet?

18" X 24" tagboard and cardboard.
Two identical sets of materials glued to 3" X 5" pieces of heavy cardboard; one set then is glued to the answerboard:

elastic	packing plastic	sandpaper	wire screening
macaroni	air bubble	heavy plastic	satin
velvet	sponge	corrugated paper	braille

Container for the second set of objects.
Blindfold.

Large-Small

Skills Learning to read the words "large" and "small"; making comparisons of size; observing and describing length, width, height, circumference, and depth; classifying according to size.

The child sorts the objects according to their size and places them on the "large" or "small" side of the answerboard. After experience with this activity a child will be ready to try a more abstract task. The teacher may want to make another game for large and small with pictures of things glued down. In this case there might be two different animals opposite one another or two kinds of tools or two types of food. The child looks at the two things and decides which one of the two would be the larger in real life. For example, there might be a hammer on one side and a screwdriver on the other. The child would indicate the hammer as the larger of the two.

The teacher might discuss the activity as follows: "What do you think this word says? And this one? Good. Now, find two things that are the same except for their size. Which side will this one go on? Why? How about this one?"

What can you tell me about the dominos? In what way is this one bigger? What about its length—are they the same length? Okay, then if this one's longer, what about this other one? Yes! It's shorter. Good.

What about the apples? What's the difference between them? What else can you say about them? This one's smaller in what way?

What about these two things? What's the difference in their size?

2' X 4' vinyl plastic with a line drawn down the center.
Two different sizes of each object used: one large and one small.
Container for objects.

MATERIALS

Classification 99

Materials

The child sorts the objects under the various categories to show the materials with which each is made.

A child who does this activity with ease may enjoy making a scrapbook of things made of different materials. He can copy one word on each page from the answerboard and paste pictures under the various headings.

The teacher might discuss the activity as follows: "Pick up one of these things and feel the material. Look at it closely. Do you know what it is made of?" (If the child does not know, the teacher holds the object in front of each word on the answerboard and asks, "Is it made of wood?" or, "Is it made of metal?" . . . until the child finds the material.)

Name all the things made of metal. The things made of wood.
Show me something made of glass that is used at Christmas.
Of what material are the things in the fourth pie tin from the left?
What is the same about things made of glass?
Show me some things that are hard. Some things that stretch. Some things that will break.
Where does leather come from? Rubber? Wood?
Are any parts of your clothing made of metal? Of wood? Of plastic? Of leather?

Six 9″ × 12″ pieces of heavy cardboard taped together.
Marking pen for writing the name of each material.
Small pieces of wood, glass, metal, rubber, plastic, and leather to glue to the answerboard.
Objects made of
  Wood: clothespin, tongue depressor, pencil, button, spool, match, twig, wheel
  Glass: jar, mirror, Christmas tree bulb, flashbulb
  Metal: can, paper clip, screw, nail, bottle cap, metal foil, button, pen, empty film spool
  Rubber: rubber band, balloon, medicine dropper top, ball, rubber cement (sealed shut)
  Plastic: straw, spool, spoon, toothbrush, comb, toy, button, ball
  Leather: wallet, belt, hide, key ring, button, child's shoe
Six metal pie tins.
Container for objects, answerboard, and pie tins.

Color Sort

The child takes the cards and sorts them according to their colors. Children should be allowed to arrange their groups in any way they wish. Some will work in rows, others in columns, and still others in areas.

By changing the cards at the top of the board the teacher can create different games. For example, the categories might be beginning sounds and the child would sort the cards by their first sounds. Other possible categories might be food, animals, and man-made things or things larger than the child, things smaller than the child and things about the child's size.

ACTIVITY

The teacher might say, "Put the pictures that are the same color together."

GETTING STARTED

Tell me about the brown things.

Do you have a favorite color? What is the picture, third from the bottom, under your favorite color?

How many yellow pictures are there? Are there more blue ones?

Without looking, can you remember three pictures under the green card? Can you remember three under the red?

IDEAS FOR
FOLLOW-UP DISCUSSION

Great care should be taken to *ask the child* why he placed pictures the way he did. What is important is that the child have a reason for his placements. For example, he may place the pepper outline under red because that is the color of pepper his mother always uses, or the bananas under brown because he likes to eat them that way, or the apple under yellow or green because he has seen different kinds.

Pocket chart.

3″ × 5″ cards.

Outline pictures of objects that are usually a particular color.

Rubber cement.

Clear contact paper to cover pictures.

Construction paper squares of eight different colors, glued on tagboard and covered with clear contact paper.

Reference sheet.

Container for cards and color squares.

MATERIALS

The Button Game

Skills Developing classification skills; sorting according to similarities and differences in color, shape, texture, and size.

The child sorts the buttons into piles. (The child should be encouraged to think of his own criteria by which to sort.)

Several similar workjobs can be made with different sets of buttons. One might have buttons similar in color, style, and size but different in texture. Another set might be buttons of the same color but a different size, or style. Still another might be a random set that the child may sort according to shape or size or whatever criterion he chooses.

A child also could sort by texture if blindfolded. In this case only a few buttons should be included.

The teacher might discuss the activity as follows: "Tell me something you notice about these buttons, Isaac." (Color, size, shape, material, number of holes, etc.) "Will you put all the buttons like that together? What will you do with the ones left over?"

Tell me how you grouped these buttons.
Why did you put these buttons here? And here? Could you have put this button here? Why? Why not?
How many buttons are in this group?
If I mixed these buttons up, what else besides their color (or whatever criterion the child has used in sorting) could you tell me about these buttons? How else could you group them?

Apple crate separator.
100 buttons in matched sets of 5 or 10.
Container for buttons.

Classification

106   *Language*

The child sorts the pictures into groups by placing similar things together. Many similar activities can be provided for children that give
them more experience with classification and forming subgroups. Children can group shades of colors by the main colors. Paint stores have
strips showing different shades, which can be cut apart and mounted on
cards for this purpose. Children can group different sizes and types of
geometric shapes, and also enjoy sorting the letters of the alphabet
according to their similar properties.

All these experiences provide for growth in logical thinking, an area
that cannot be overstressed in the school day.

The teacher might say, "Look through the pictures and put the ones
that are the same in some way together."

Tell me about the pictures in each pile.
What do you call all these things?
Are there any animal names you do *not* know?
Can you take the pictures in this pile and divide them up still further?
Are there any things you could put together? (Toys I'd like for
Christmas, toys I don't want; food I like to eat, food I don't like;
clothes for a girl, clothes for a boy; animals that scare me, animals I'd
like for pets.)

Pictures cut from old workbooks mounted on 3″ x 5″ cards: 10 pictures of
clothing, 10 pictures of toys, 10 pictures of animals, 10 pictures of food.
Clear contact paper to protect pictures.
Container for pictures.

Note: Other groups of pictures can be used in similar workjobs—for example,
bathroom furniture, bedroom furniture, kitchen furniture, and living room furniture. Cars, trucks, trains, and airplanes are especially appealing to the boys.

Sounds and Letters

Sound Boxes

Skills Developing auditory perception; discriminating between similar sounds; making selections; matching.

110   *Language*

The child sorts the containers according to the sound made when he shakes them, placing each identical pair on an answerboard.

ACTIVITY

The teacher might discuss the activity as follows: "Shake this box and listen to how it sounds. Can you find the box that sounds exactly like this one? Good. Put them together on an answerboard. Can you find another pair?

GETTING STARTED

Tell me how you did your work, Patricia.
Which pair makes the least amount of sound? Which one makes the harshest sound? The softest? Which is the most pleasing to you?
Which pair was the easiest for you to find? Was there one which was hard to find?
What do you think might be in this pair? Could it be rocks? Could it be feathers? Why?
Which pair has a sound which you might hear at a swimming pool, washing dishes, or in the bathtub?
How many pairs jingle?
How can you describe the sounds of these pairs?

IDEAS FOR
FOLLOW-UP DISCUSSION

Tagboard cut into squares.
Felt marking pen.
Empty school milk cartons.
Two each: 1/2 cup rice, 1/2 cup salt or sand, sets of jingle bells, sets of pennies, small balls, 1 cup of water, 1/4 cup beans, "moo" toys.
Masking tape to seal boxes.
Spray paint.
Container for cards and boxes.

MATERIALS

Alphabet Train

Skills Pairing capital and small letters of the alphabet; selecting first sounds of words; experiencing alphabetical order; strengthening left-to-right progression.

The child takes the objects and puts them into the alphabet train according to their beginning sound. The "cat" goes into the car marked "c," the rat goes into the one marked "r," and so forth.

The teacher might discuss this activity as follows: "Choose one object from the box. What is it? What sound does it begin with? What letter does it begin with? Can you find that letter on the alphabet train? Yes, there it is! What about this next object?"

What word starts with the letter "s"? The letter "c"? The letter "m"?
What sound does "fork" begin with? Where would a "man" go in the alphabet train? Where would a "pen" go?
How many letters are there in the alphabet? How many letters are after "s"? After "x"?
What letter comes between "a" and "c"? Between "n" and "p"?
Show me a short letter. A tall one. A wiggly one. A straight one. One with a dot over itself.
Name two letters at the beginning of the alphabet. One at the end.
Show me all the letters that are in your name.

26 small milk cartons with the tops cut off.
Colored paper in various colors to cover the cartons.
Clear contact paper to cover the colored paper.
Marking pen to write the letters of the alphabet on the cars.
Small cardboard circles for wheels.
Brass fasteners to attach wheels to cars.
Yarn to link the 26 cars together.
Engine.
Two or more objects beginning with each sound of the alphabet to go inside the train car; for example, *a*pple, *a*nchor, *b*ed, *b*one, *c*at, *c*ar, *d*oll, *d*uck.
Container for objects.
Container for train and boxed objects.

Phonics Boards

Skills Developing auditory perception; selecting beginning sounds; reproducing sounds; classifying according to the first sound in words; learning names of objects.

The child says the name of each object and circles all the ones that begin with a particular sound. The teacher and the child decide together which of the three sounds the child will listen to.

The teacher might discuss the activity as follows: "What sound would you like to listen for this time, Starlette?—'mmmm', 'ssss', or 't'? Okay, let's see if you can find something that begins like 'mmmm.' Say the names of the pictures: 'soap'—does that begin like 'mmmm'? How about this one?—'table'—does that begin like 'mmm'? How about this one then—'mountain.' Does that begin like 'mmm'? Good for you, Starlette! Put one of the rings around it. See if you can find the others by yourself."

What sound were you listening for?
Let's say the names of all the things that start like that.
How many rings did you use for this workjob?
Does your name begin like this sound? How about mine? What *is* the first sound in your name?

18" x 24" tagboard and cardboard.
10 pictures for each beginning sound.
Rubber cement.
Clear contact paper to protect answerboard.
Masking tape to strengthen all edges.
10 plastic bracelets or rings cut from heavy plastic.
Container for bracelets or rings.

Note: Several different games can be made, each with a different set of three sounds. (By grouping the sounds in threes, the child can use the same answerboard three separate times, selecting a different sound each time.)

Phonics Arrow Game

Skills Developing auditory perception; listening for and selecting first sounds in words; reproducing sounds; naming pictures of objects; associating sound and symbol.

116   *Language*

ACTIVITY

The child takes the phonics cards and looks at the letter whose sound he is to listen for. Then he names the pictures at the bottom of the card and finds the one he is looking for. He turns the arrow to the picture whose beginning sound matches the letter at the top of the card. When he has finished, the child turns the arrows back to the letters.

GETTING STARTED

The teacher might discuss the activity as follows: "What sound does this letter make? Let's say the names of each of the pictures at the bottom and find which one begins with the sound of 'sss.' (They name the pictures.) Now, which one starts like 't'? Fine. Can you do the next one?"

IDEAS FOR FOLLOW-UP DISCUSSION

What sound were you listening for?
Let's say the names of the pictures you turned the arrow to and listen for that sound. Can you fix this mistake? Good!

MATERIALS

Eight squares of tagboard, cardboard, and clear contact paper.
Eight arrows cut from tagboard and covered with clear contact paper.
Masking tape to strengthen edges.
Pictures of the sound to be listened for.
Pictures of other sounds among which the child is to discriminate.
Container for cards.

Note: Secure the arrows with the brass fasteners to the tagboard before backing it with cardboard. This prevents the brass fasteners from pulling out with use.

A set of cards can be made for each beginning sound. A set of cards can also be made for selecting sound *anywhere* in the word. For example, the child may be asked to listen for the sound of "sss" and be given pictures of a cat, a horse, and a table. The child who is ready may be asked to indicate the position of the sound in the word. A number 1 might designate the beginning position, number 2, the middle, and number 3, the end.

First-Sound Sorting Boxes

The child sorts the objects into the boxes matching the initial sound of each object with the appropriate letter.

The teacher might discuss the activity as follows: "Pick up one of the objects from the box. What is it? Does that word start like this—'rrrr'—(pointing to the box with the 'r' on it)? Does it start like 'nn' (pointing to that letter)? Does it start like 'd'? Yes! Let's say it together. Can you hear that first sound of 'd'? Put it in the box. Now, take the next object and see if you can find this one yourself."

Say the names of the things in the "nnn" box. Do they all begin with "nnn"?

Show me something beginning with "rrr" that could help a person draw a straight line. Something hard. Something cold inside.

Show me something beginning with "nnn" that you could eat. Something you could mend a rip with. Something you could use to catch a goldfish with.

Show me something beginning with "ddd" you could buy something with.

Three boxes, each designated with one letter.
Spray paint.
Objects to be sorted according to their initial sounds;
   r: rock, ruler, raisins, robot, refrigerator, rocker, rice
   n: net, notebook, needle, nine, necklace, nuts, nail
   d: dove, desk, devil, dog, dime, doll, dish
Container for objects.
Container for boxes and boxed objects.

Peek a Boo Word Game

Skills Strengthening visual memory; observing the position of letters in words; learning to read; reproducing words from a pattern; strengthening left-to-right progression.

The child "peeks" under the picture by lifting up the tab and sees the letters that spell the word. Then he takes the letters and "spells" out the word by placing the letters in the transparency pockets.

The teacher might discuss the activity.as follows: "What is this a picture of? Do you know how to spell this word? Peek under the picture and see what letters you will need. (Child looks.) Can you find those letters? Only peek when you *really* need to—try to stretch your memory!!"

(Looking at a word where the letters are not in the correct order) What does this word say? Let's look under the picture and check to be sure the letters are in the right order. (Child looks.) Are they exactly the same? Can you fix it?

I see a mistake in this word, Moses. Can you find it and fix it?

How many words are there?

Can you tell me what letter "horses" begins with?

Which one is the shortest?

Can you tell me which word is the longest—has the most letters in it? Which one is the shortest?

Which is your favorite picture? Practice for a while on this word and see if you can walk to the board at the front of the room and write the word without forgetting the order of the letters.

18″ X 24″ tagboard and cardboard.
Eight transparencies cut into 9″ X 3″ strips.
Cloth tape.
Pictures of familiar objects glued to 3″ X 3″ squares of tagboard hinged with cloth tape to a second 3″ X 3″ square and glued to answerboard.
Marking pen to write words under pictures and on cards.
3″ X 1-1/2″ strips of lightweight cardboard with letters written on them.
Container for letters.

Supermarket

ACTIVITY-CENTERED LEARNING FOR K–2 MATHEMATICS
Books by Mary Baratta-Lorton

WORKJOBS II
Number Activities for Early Childhood

MATHEMATICS THEIR WAY
An Activity-Centered Mathematics Program for Early Childhood Education

Twenty open-ended math activities which encourage children to explore the concept of number through concrete experiences. Children progress from the concrete to the abstract level of number while captivating objects and creatures made from ordinary items stimulate their young imaginations. **Each activity is used over and over at higher levels of skill development.**

WORKJOBS II PROVIDES:

- materials lists and instructions for assembling the activities
- blackline masters for worksheets, gameboards, numeral and equation cards
- discussion of the "their-way" philosophy
- classroom management techniques for individualizing

WORKJOBS II CAN BE EFFECTIVELY USED WITH ANY BASAL MATH PROGRAM

An exciting activity-centered mathematics curriculum designed *especially* for K–2 use. *Mathematics THEIR Way* may be used as a completely self-contained math program or as an activity supplement to enrich any basal math series.

- Shows how children develop mathematical understanding through activities using familiar materials.
- Contains over 200 *classroom-tested and proven* experiences, with 600 illustrative photographs.
- Includes sample teaching strategies, with possible student/teacher dialogue where appropriate.
- Answers typical questions that teachers have asked about classroom problems and planning.
- Pictures all materials and shows how they can be made or obtained.
- Provides a complete, easy-to-use assessment program.
- Includes a blackline master pad for duplicating 61 worksheets, 9 observation forms, and 16 skill assessment sheets.

Now young children can have valuable WORKJOBS experiences *at home* ... with Mary Baratta-Lorton's

WORKJOBS ... for Parents
Activity-Centered Learning in the Home

52 Workjob activities from the original WORKJOBS selected as especially suited for parents to use with young children at home ... PLUS several newly developed activities.

WORKJOBS ... for Parents provides a series of manipulative tasks inexpensively made from readily-available materials. Included for each activity are:

- list of skills developed
- suggestions for starting
- list of materials needed
- photograph of children working with the activities
- ideas for follow-up discussion

The book also features a discussion of how to best use activity-centered learning in the home.

Special note: Home-based activities from *WORKJOBS ... for Parents* can further enrich the learning experiences of children doing Workjobs at school ... and teachers can multiply their time effectiveness by arranging for parents to lend their home-fabricated Workjobs materials.

FOR MORE INFORMATION ON **WORKJOBS ... FOR PARENTS**, CHECK THE APPROPRIATE BOX ON THE REVERSE AND RETURN THIS CARD.

The child takes the objects and sorts them into the bags according to their first sound.

The teacher, pointing to the letters on the outside of the bags, might ask, "How does this letter sound? And this one? Can you find the objects that will go into each bag? How about this—what is it? Does it begin with this sound? With this one? Then where will you put it? Do the next one while I watch."

Show me something you might eat for breakfast. What sound does it begin with?

Is there something hard? What do you do with it? What is it's first sound?

What do you put on a sandwich? What kind of a sandwich would you use it on? What sound does it begin with?

Show me something that begins with the same sound as Michael's name.

Close your eyes. Name as many things as you can that you put in the "sss" bag. Good for you, Lisa. Now let's check.

Three paper bags with a letter written on the outside.
A series of objects whose names begin with the sounds on the bags.
Container for objects.
Container for the bags and boxed objects.

MATERIALS

Note: Similar games can be made for other beginning sounds where the letter is written on an object such as clothing, birds, buttons, or car engines. The child then matches these with corresponding objects such as clothes lines, nests, shirts, or cars which are identified with the appropriate beginning sounds.

Animal Cages

Skills Developing auditory perception; identifying and reproducing beginning sounds in words; associating sound and symbol.

The child says the name of the animal and listens for the beginning sound. He places the animals in the appropriate cages according to the beginning sound.

The children should have an understanding of beginning sounds and be familiar with the names of the animals they will use before they begin this workjob.

The teacher might ask the child, "What is the name of this animal? What sound does it begin with? Can you find the letter which makes that sound and put the animal in that cage?"

Show me an animal whose name begins with the sound of "l".

If I were going to write down the word "rhinocerous," which letter would I write first? How about "tiger"? Or "walrus"?

Name the animals for me.

Show me an animal that lives in the trees. One that loves to swim. One that is very large and heavy.

If I gave you a turtle, which cage would he go in? What if I gave you a cat? A leopard?

One toy animal of each kind: deer, monkey, rhinocerous, lion, tiger, camel, zebra, bear, gorilla, hippopotamus, fox, seal, walrus.

Empty strawberry baskets with one letter affixed to each: *d m r l t c z b g h f s w.*

Container for animals.

Container for boxed animals and "cages."

Note: If three baskets are stacked and taped together the "cages" will be very sturdy.

Numeral cards
should be available
to any children who
need them when
working with
mathematics activities.

THE DEVELOPMENT OF MATHEMATICS THROUGH WORKJOBS

Mathematics is *living—life*—not rote drill with meaningless symbols and still more meaningless "answers." Mathematics is going shopping for a dozen eggs and three pounds of sweet potatoes, or sharing your candy bar among five friends, or collecting three tons of old newspapers for the Scout paper drive. Mathematics is sorting clothes on washday, or dividing a soft drink for you and your sister so it's "fair." Mathematics is saving a nickel a week out of your allowance to buy that great kite you saw at the drugstore, or figuring out how much material to buy to make a minidress from this maxi pattern you've got, or trying to guess how many more sprigs of ivy you're going to need to plant the rest of the embankment.

Every child comes to school with a rich background for mathematical understanding. This background is as yet unorganized in the child's mind, but it is a rich resource for a teacher who wishes to help the child gain a real and lasting understanding of numbers and all their varied relationships.

The activities in this section have as their main goal *understanding,* not computation or memory. They are intended to assist the child in organizing the mathematics in the world around him. He handles familiar objects and sees sets of objects that he can count. He learns number facts through experience, not by memory. In this way, he will grow to see mathematics as natural and significant, and symbolization and computation as a way of writing down his experiences so they can be shared.

127

Sets

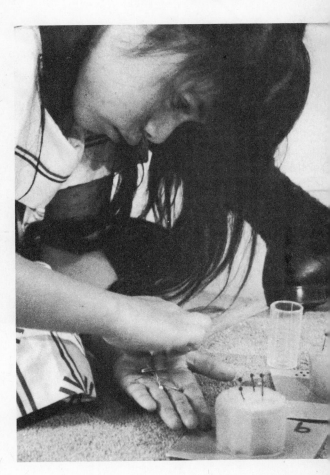

Pincushions

The child puts the appropriate number of pins into the pincushions. He then orders them 1 through 10.

The teacher might ask the child, "How many pins would you stick into this pincushion? Why?"

What did you do with the pins and pincushions?
Show me the pins you like best. What color are they?
Count the pins in the pincushion with the numeral 9 on it. How many are left?
Without doing it yet, how many pins do you think would be left from the pincushion with numeral 7 on it if you removed six of the pins? Take them away and see if you are right.

3" squares of cardboard.
Pincushion shapes cut from
  foam rubber.
Glue.
Spray paint.
55 large-headed pins.
Container for pins.
Container for pincushions
  and boxed pins.

The Safety Pin Game

The child fastens the appropriate number of pins to the material.

The teacher might ask, "How many pins will you pin onto this piece of material, Antoinette? Why?"

What have you been doing, Antoinette?
What are these called? What are safety pins made of?
Count the pins on this material, please.
What color is this material?
Do you have any clothes this same color? What?
Does anyone in our classroom have this color on right now?

Felt or material pieces, approximately the size of the box used.
Large safety pins.
Felt marking pen to write numerals on the felt.
Container for pins.
Container for felt and boxed pins.

MATERIALS

Easter Baskets

The child fills each basket with the appropriate number of "eggs" and orders the baskets from 1 through 10. When the work has been checked, the child places the cup of cereal in his desk until recess when he may eat it!

A child who is ready may enjoy placing two baskets together and recording the combinations formed.

The teacher might ask the child, "How many Easter eggs will you put in this basket? And this one?"

Tell me what you've been working on.

How did you go about doing this work?

Show me a basket that has the same number of eggs as we have doors in our room. Show me a basket that has the same number of eggs as my car has wheels. Show me a numeral that tells how many teeth you have missing in the front of your mouth.

How many eggs do you have in this basket? (Child counts.) What number is on the front of the basket? Are there that many eggs? (If not) Can you fix it so there are that many eggs?

If you eat three eggs from this basket, how many eggs would you have left? Eat them and let's see.

If you dump the eggs in this basket with these others, how many would you have?

10 small Easter baskets.
Plastic Easter grass, enough to fill each basket.
White, clear-drying glue to mix with grass before filling baskets so the grass will stick to the basket.
Writing pen for writing numerals.
Small cups of sugar-coated cereal (of different colors) to look like Easter eggs.
Container for baskets.

Note: The cereal can be kept in a covered container on the teacher's desk or some other convenient place with a supply of small cups. When the child is ready for this activity he knows where the cereal is and can get what he needs.

Number Lines

The child inserts the appropriate number of golf tees into each number line and orders them from 1 through 10.

The teacher might discuss the activity as follows: "What does this number tell you? Can you put that many golf tees into the number line? Good!"

Explain a little bit about what you did with this workjob, please.
Can you put these in order, starting with number 1? What number will come first? What will come after that?
Which number is the same as your age?
Which number line has the most golf tees in it? Which one has the fewest?
Which number line has more golf tees than three but not as many as five?
How many holes are not filled up on this number line? And on this one?
Is there a number line that does not have *any* holes filled up?
Is there a number line that has *all* its holes filled up?

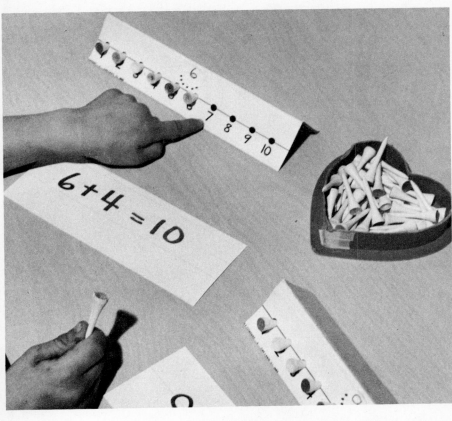

Some children may enjoy recording the combinations adding up to ten on each number line.

10 number lines from 1 through 10 made of heavy paper and mounted on cardboard with the holes punched out.
Colored golf tees.
Marking pen for writing the numerals.
Container for golf tees.
Container for number lines and boxed golf tees.

Number Boards

The child counts the dots or notes the numeral to determine the number of nails to band on each board. The block with the numeral 7, for example, will have a rubber band around 7 nails.

The teacher might discuss the activity as follows: "What does this numeral tell you? What could you have done if you weren't sure what the numeral was? Where are the dots? Show me, please. Okay, good. Now, what was this numeral again? Put a rubber band around that many nails. Very good. Do the next one."

Tell me about this work, Christine.
Why did you put the rubber band around this many nails?
Show me a board with fewer than four nails circled.
Point to all the boards that have five nails circled.
Put all the boards with fewer than three nails circled on the left side of the table, and those with three or more than three nails circled on the right side.
Show me a board with one more than two nails circled.
Show me a board that shows none circled. What do we call this numeral?

A child may use some nails on the top line and some nails on the bottom line. After talking with his teacher the child may be asked if he would like to record these combinations.

Pieces of wood 3″ x 6″.
10 finishing nails for each board.
Numeral cards with a number dot card hinged underneath.
Small, but strong, colored rubber bands.
Container for rubber bands.
Container for wooden blocks and boxed rubber bands.

Math Recording Game

Skills Forming sets of objects; counting; learning to record experience with mathematical symbols; reading; making comparisons.

The child records with pictures and words what he sees on each answer-card, and fills in the missing numeral.

The teacher might discuss the activity as follows: "How many spools are on your paper. What does this word say? Why is it written here? Could you use it to tell about the spools? Where would be a good place to write it on your paper? That's fine job. Let me see you do this next one."

Tell me about your workjob.
What did you write on your paper? How did you know what to write? Where did you find the words to use? What do these words tell about?
Show me the answercard that your paper tells about. Read your paper to me, please.
Show me with your fingers what this numeral you've written means. Are you holding up the same number of fingers as the numeral represents?
Are there more spools or more fingers, or what? Why?

6″ x 6″ squares of cardboard.
Objects to form sets.
Marking pen.
Epoxy glue.
Paper.
Crayons.
Container for cards.

"I Counted"

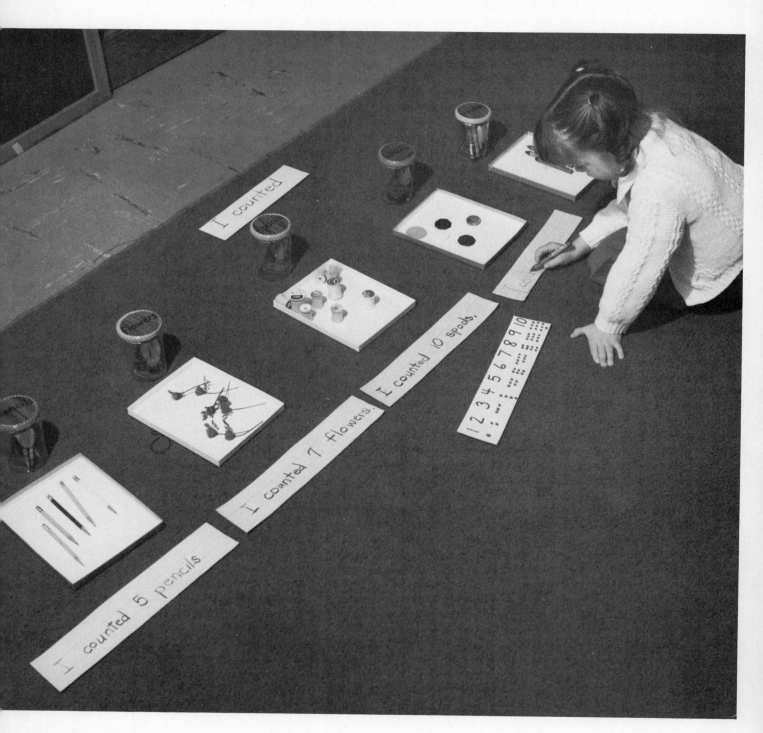

I counted

I counted 10 spools.

I counted 7 flowers.

I counted 5 pencils.

flowers

pencil

1 2 3 4 5 6 7 8 9 10

The child puts out the boxes and places some objects into each box. He takes a piece of paper and writes the number of objects he counted, copying the label on the container to show *what* he counted.

The teacher might discuss the activity as follows: "Put some things in each box from the containers. (Later) Take some paper and write what you did." (Pointing to the words the teacher might say) "This says, 'I counted.' How many things did you count into the box? Write that number and then write what you counted." If the child says he can't write the word the teacher suggests, "Is the word written anywhere so that you could copy it? Yes, on the label! Let's read the sentence together . . . Try the next one now."

What have you been doing?
Tell me about each box and read the sentences for me.
Show me the word "pencils." Show me the word "blocks." Can you close your eyes and spell "blocks?"
How many rubber bands do you have in this box?
What do you have the most of? Do you have the same number of any items? What are they?
Do you have more pencils in the box where you counted them out or are there more pencils left in this container?
What do you have three of? Seven of? Nine of?

Some children may enjoy placing a small paper bag over each jar and guessing how many items are left. The child knows there were 10 items in each jar to start with, so if there are five items in the box, there must be five left in the covered jar.

Eight to 10 shallow (nylon stocking) boxes.
Sets of 10 objects such as pencils, toys, nuts (in shells), old toothbrushes, blocks, large rubber bands, small jars. (Each set is in a separate labeled container.)
A label stating, "I counted."
Paper and pencil.
Small paper bags.
Large container for sets of objects and stocking boxes.

Flannelboard Groups

The child takes the flannelboard pieces to the flannelboard, sorts them into like sets, counts the members in each set and applies the appropriate numeral.

The teacher might discuss the activity as follows: "Put all the shapes that are the same together. Then find the numeral that tells how many shapes are in each set and put the numeral by the set of shapes it goes with."

What did you do with the flannel shapes? How did you group them?
How many groups are there? How many numerals are there?
How many apples are in this set? Count them for me.
Show me a set of shapes with more shapes than you have fingers on one hand. How many shapes are there in this set? What numeral tells about this number? What is it called?
What shape are the things in the set of six? In the set of three?
What color are the stars? How many are there?
Which set has more in it, the set of birds or the set of apples?
Which set has the most objects? What has the least? Which numeral shows the most? Which shows the least?

Flannelboard.
Flannel shapes (six patterns with a varying number of each).
Flannel numerals, cut out, to check on reversals (with number dots on the back to make them self-correcting).
Container for flannel shapes and numerals.

Number Dots

Skills Forming sets of objects; counting; learning to record experience with mathematical symbols; one-to-one correspondence.

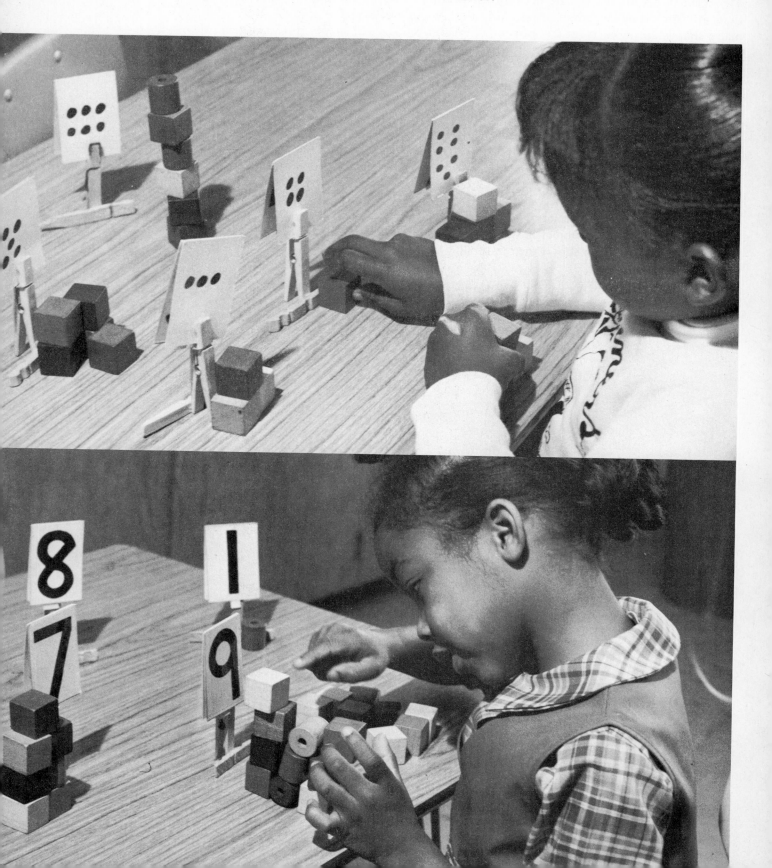

A child takes the numeral card stands and some blocks and "builds" the number in front of each set of dots or numeral.

When a child works easily and competently with the numerals 1 through 9, he can begin working with commercial or homemade place value blocks. A unit block is 3/4" square, a 10s block is 7-1/2" long by 3/4".

The teacher might discuss the activity as follows: "Put this many blocks (pointing to a numeral) in front of this stand, Valerie. How can you find out what numeral it is? Yes, count the dots to be sure! How many blocks are here? And what numeral is this? Are there the same number of blocks as dots? Let me know when you've finished building!"

Tell me how you did this work, Valerie.

How many blocks are in this pile? Why are there just that number? Couldn't you have put two more here? Why not?

Point to the numeral that shows this many (holding up a number of fingers). What is that numeral called?

When he is ready, the child can begin working with place value.

1" cubes.
Clothespin stands made by glueing half a clothespin at the bottom of a complete one.
Cards for writing dots or numerals.
Container for numeral cards.
Container for blocks.

Trees and Apples

Skills Forming sets of objects; counting; making comparisons; combining groups.

The child places apples on each tree until the amount matches the numeral on the tree trunk.

The teacher might ask the child, "What is this numeral, Marlvin? Are there that many apples on the tree? Can you fix it so there are enough apples?"

What did you do with the apples?
How many apples are on this tree?
Are there more trees or more apples?
These two trees have how many apples between them?
Which tree has the fewest apples? The most?
How many apples would need to fall down to leave only two apples on
    this tree?
I see a mistake on this tree. Do you see it? Can you fix it?

Tagboard piece 6″ x 9″.
Marking pen in brown to make tree trunks.
Self-adhesive labels on which to write numerals.
Green felt to make tree tops.
Apples cut from red felt.
Container for apples.
Container for answerboards and boxed apples.

The Number Cans

Skills One-to-one correspondence; forming sets of objects; counting; ordering numerically; making comparisons; combining groups; subtracting, withdrawing a part from a whole.

The child puts the necessary number of tongue depressors into each can or carton.

The teacher might discuss the activity as follows: "These dots tell you how many sticks to put into the can, Eric. Try this one. Very good, Eric. That's exactly right. Try another one."

Explain to me, please, what you did with the sticks.
How did you know how many sticks to put in this box? Show me how you did it. What if you had put in only one stick instead of three? Would that have been okay? Why?
Count the sticks in this can, please.

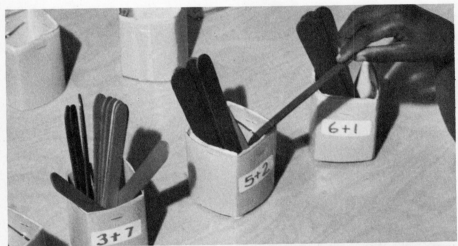

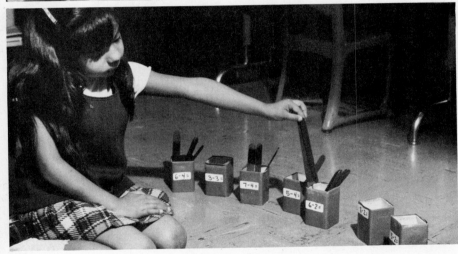

*Children who are
ready may work
on addition and
subtraction problems.*

Empty orange juice cans or milk cartons painted with spray paint.
Tongue depressor sticks, painted with spray paint.
Round adhesive labels.
Container for tongue depressors.
Container for cans and boxed sticks.

Note: The tongue depressors resist soil and remain attractive for years if spray painted.

Select-a-Set

The child counts the set in each picture and matches it with the appropriate numeral. If the child counts five apples, for example, he puts the picture under the numeral 5.

The teacher might discuss the activity as follows: "Take a card and count the pictures. Good. How many flags are there, Carol? Where do you think it should go? Why? Good thinking!"

What numerals have you been working with?
Tell me what you did with the cards.
Are there enough balls in this picture to give one to each person in our class? How many children could have one?
Show me a card that does not have animals or people on it. What do you call these pictures?
Show me a card with five of something to eat. With three things you could smell. With four things you could hold in one hand.

When a child is ready to work with addition, he may place two cards together and record their sum.

Pocket chart.
Pictures cut from arithmetic workbooks showing sets of objects: 10 sets of one, 10 sets of two, 10 sets of three, 10 sets of four, 10 sets of five.
50 3″ x 5″ index cards for mounting pictures.
Rubber cement.
Clear contact paper to protect pictures.
Numerals 1, 2, 3, 4, and 5, written on tagboard and covered with clear contact paper.
Container for cards.

Cereal Game

The child fills a paper cup with cereal. Then he counts the number of pieces of cereal required into the depressions in the apple separator.
When the child has had his work checked, he puts the cereal back into his paper cup and puts it where he may get it at recess or snack time and eat it!

The teacher might ask the child, "How many pieces of cereal will you put here? And here?"

How did you decide where to put the cereal?

Do you have any cereal left in your cup? How many pieces? How many would you have to eat to have just three pieces left? Try it and see if you're right.

How many pieces of cereal should you put here? Count and tell me if you have enough. Good! Now, how about this one? Can you fix it?

If we were to put these pieces from this group together with these pieces here, how many would we have? Show me.

If you have five (indicating a group of five pieces of cereal) and add one more, how many do you have?

If you have seven (indicating a group of seven) and you take three away, how many do you have?

Separator from an apple crate.
Marking pen to write numerals and combinations.
Small cup of cereal.

Note: The cereal can be kept in a covered container on the teacher's desk or some other convenient place with a supply of small cups. When the child is ready for this activity he knows where the cereal is and can get what he needs.

The teacher controls the difficulty of this task by the numerals she puts in the cups. Some teachers may want to make several games—one with numbers 1 to 5, one with numbers 1 to 9, and one with addition and subtraction combinations.

Hangers and Clothes Pins

Skills Forming sets of objects; counting; ordering numerically.

The child puts the appropriate number of clothespins on the hangers and orders them from 1 through 10.

ACTIVITY

The teacher might ask the child, "How many clothespins will you put on this hanger? And this one?"

GETTING STARTED

IDEAS FOR
FOLLOW-UP DISCUSSION

Tell me about your work and what you've been doing, Howard.

Why did you put six clothespins on this hanger?

How many red clothespins are on this hanger? How many altogether?

Let's write down how many of each color you have on this hanger. First take a red crayon. How many red clothespins are there? Can you write that? (Child writes the number or makes dots or lines depending on his readiness.) And how many yellow pins are there? What color will you use to write that many? And how many green? How many are there all together?

Which hanger has the most clothespins on it? Which one has the least? Which one has the same number as your age? As you have fingers on two hands? As you have noses?

10 clothes hangers.

Colored plastic clothespins or spray painted wooden pins in four colors.

Tagboard cut into 3″ X 5″ strips covered with clear contact paper after writing numerals.

Stapler to affix numeral cards to clothes hangers.

Something in the classroom to hang the hangers on.

Container for clothespins.

Container for hangers and boxed clothespins.

MATERIALS

The Odd Ball

The child looks for the "odd ball," the set that does *not* match the numeral, and crosses it out.

The teacher might discuss the activity as follows: "Most of these are the same, but there is one set on each page that does not belong. Can you find which one is the 'odd ball' and be ready to tell me why it doesn't belong?"

Why is this set the "odd ball"? How many are in this set?
How many sets are the same on this card? How many odd balls are there?
What would have to be done to this "odd ball" to make it have the necessary number?

9" X 12" tagboard.
Pictures of various sets of objects.
Rubber cement for pasting pictures to the tagboard.
Masking tape to strengthen edges.
Xs cut from heavy paper.
Container for Xs.
Container for cards and boxed Xs.

Note: On each sheet, paste sets of the same quantity except for one. That set may be fewer or more in quantity, and it is the set the children are looking for.

Piggy Banks

Skills Forming sets of objects; counting; making comparisons; learning about money; developing respect for property; combining groups.

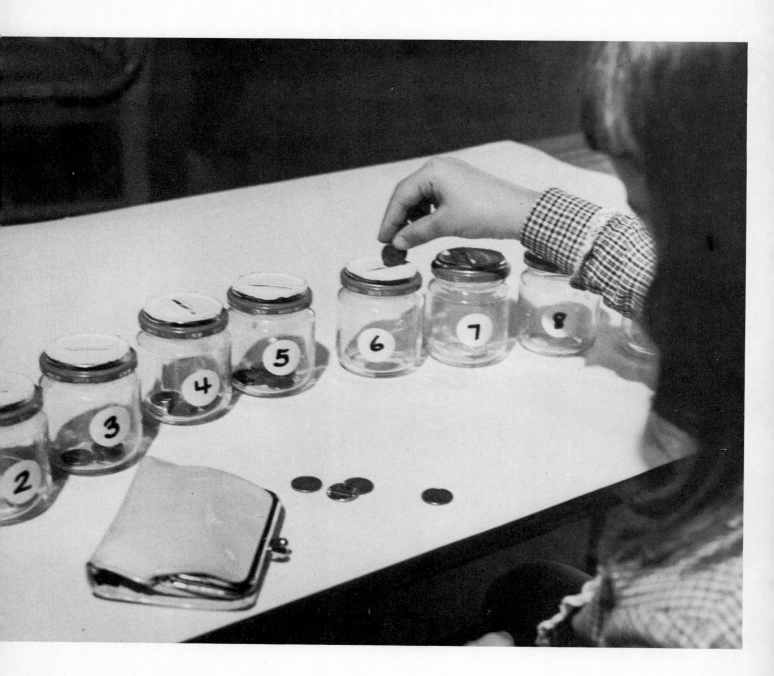

The child drops the appropriate number of pennies or disks into each "piggy bank." For instance, in the bank marked "9" he drops in nine pennies, and in the one marked "3" he drops in three.

The teacher might ask the child: "How many pennies will you put into this bank? Why?"

What did you do with the pennies and jars?
Could you put the banks in order from 1 through 10?
Which bank has the most money in it? The least?
If you wanted to buy a piece of penny bubble gum, which bank would you get the money out of?
If I wanted you to give me six cents from *two* banks, which two would you use? How about eight cents? Four cents?
If you wanted to buy a balloon for four cents, which bank would you take the money from?
Show me a bank that has the same number of pennies as your age.
Count all the pennies and tell me how many there are.

10 baby food jars with lids.
Screwdriver to punch slots in lids.
Sticker numerals glued to jars.
Cloth tape for covering the jagged metal of the slots.
Pennies, poker chips, or other small disks.
Matching board for counting the money.
Container for disks, chips, or pennies.
Container for jars.

Note: Some teachers may prefer to store the pennies in some area other than with the workjob. The child would then get the pennies when ready to begin this activity.
    See text at the end of the book for a discussion on the use of real money as opposed to play money or disks in the workjobs.

Sets 161

Cars and Garages

The child matches the dots on the car with the numeral on the garage and drives the car into its garage. The car with seven dots should drive into the garage with number 7. The one with only two dots drives into number 2.

ACTIVITY

The teacher might discuss the activity as follows: "How many dots are on this car? Count them for me, please. How many are there? Can you find a garage that this car can drive into? Why do you think the car goes into this particular garage? Very good. Where do you think this car goes?"

GETTING STARTED

What did you do with the cars?

Why did you drive *this* car into *this* garage?

What is this numeral? How can you show me what numeral it is if I don't know what it is?

If I drove this car (with four dots) into this garage (with numeral 1), would it be okay? Why?

How many cars are there with three dots?

IDEAS FOR
FOLLOW-UP DISCUSSION

MATERIALS

Empty milk cartons.
Colorful construction paper covered with clear contact paper.
Numeral cards, hinged, with number dots underneath.
Small plastic cars.
Marking pen for drawing dots on the cars.
Container for cars.
Container for garages and boxed cars.

Flowers and Vases

A child puts the appropriate number of flowers (blossoms are counted, not stems) into each vase.

ACTIVITY

The teacher might discuss the activity as follows: "Choose a vase, Suzanne. How can you find out how many flowers to put into this vase? That's right; look at the numeral. How many will go into the vase you've chosen? Fine, Suzanne. Put that many blossoms into the vase. How many is that altogether? And what does the numeral say? Good. Try another one."

GETTING STARTED

Explain what you did with the flowers and vases, please.
How many flowers are in this vase?
How many blossoms are on this stem? And this one? How many is that altogether?
Point to a vase with four flowers.
Point to a vase that has less than three flowers. One with more than two flowers.
Show me a vase with the same number of flowers as fingers I am holding up.
Show me a vase that does *not* have two, three, or six flowers in it. How many is that? Could you have pointed to any other vase? How about this one? Why?
Take two flowers away from each vase, and tell me how many flowers are left in each as you do it.

IDEAS FOR
FOLLOW-UP DISCUSSION

*Children can put
two vases together
and record their sum.*

Small plastic juice bottles suitable as vases.
Marking pen.
Artificial flowers.
Container for flowers.
Container for vases and boxed flowers.

MATERIALS

Note: Plastic flowers with more than one blossom on the stem are excellent for forming combinations, as 2 + 3 or 4 + 1, and so on.

The Paper Clip Game

Skills Forming sets of objects; counting; learning to use a paper clip.

A child clips as many paper clips to each square as the numeral shows him.

When he is able to do so, the child can put two cards together and record the combinations formed.

The teacher might discuss the activity as follows: "How can you find how many paper clips to clip to this square? Good for you! Put on that many paper clips."

What did you do with the paper clips? How did you know how many to put on each square?
Tell me about this card. What does this "3" mean?
This has a mistake. Can you find it yourself and fix it?
Show me a card that has the same number of paper clips as your age. Show me a card that has less than your age. How long ago were you that old? Can you write that subtraction problem and the answer on the board?

MATERIALS

4" x 4" tagboard squares covered with clear contact paper.
Marking pen to write numerals.
Masking tape to strengthen edges.
Large paper clips.
Container for paper clips.
Container for squares and boxed paper clips.

Number Combination Board

Skills Counting; matching; making comparisons; making selections.

The child counts the set of objects on each tag and hangs it up on the appropriate hook on the answerboard.

The teacher might discuss the activity as follows: "Count the glasses on this card, Danny. How many glasses are there? Where is the numeral which shows how many there are? Check to be sure you have the right one. Hang the card up. How about the next card?"

What did you do with the cards?
How many sets of five are there?
Show me all the pictures that are in set 2. What are they pictures of?
What numeral is above the glasses? Above the stars?
Are there more ice cream cones or more kites?

The child who is ready to work with written combinations can be asked to sort cards with addition and subtraction problems.

18" X 24" plywood.
Pieces of wood 2-1/2" X 7" nailed to bottom edge of the plywood to make it stand up.
Five "L" hooks.
Five numeral cards, hinged, with number dots underneath.
Spray paint for board.
1" X 2" postage tags with hole reinforcements.
Colored pencils to draw sets or sets cut from workbooks.
Container for cards.

The Nail Board

Skills Seeing patterns and combinations; matching; forming sets of objects; making comparisons; one-to-one correspondence; making selections.

A child takes the pins and hammer, and pounds the pins into the answerboard, reproducing the various patterns.

The teacher might discuss the activity as follows: "Look at this first pattern, Carol. What colors are there? How many of each color? Take that many colored pins. Very good. Now, hammer them into the answerboard making the same pattern as you see here. Very good. Try another pattern."

Tell me what you did with the pins, Carol.

How did you know what colors to use for each pattern? Show me, please.

Point to a pattern that has three red pins in it. What other color pins does it have?

Show me a pattern that has all green pins. Is there any other pattern that has all the same color pins in it?

Show me a pattern that does not have any red pins in it.

Tell me how many pins there are altogether in some set that has red and yellow pins.

I am looking at a set that has five pins altogether, and three of the pins are green. Which one might it be? What color are the other two pins?

Do you have a favorite pattern? Why do you like it? Does it have your favorite color in it? What is it?

12" x 24" insulation board, cork, or bulletin material.
Colored marking pens for coloring patterns.
Cloth tape to strengthen all edges.
Colored pushpins, as needed to complete the patterns.
Small hammer.
Container for the hammer and pins.

Birthday Cakes

172   *Mathematics*

The child puts one birthday card in front of each cake and puts the correct number of candles on each birthday cake. The cakes may be ordered from 1 through 10.

The teacher might discuss the activity as follows: "Set a birthday card up in front of each cake. How old is the person who is going to get this cake? Can you put that many candles on his cake? Fine."

What have you been doing?
Which cake is for the youngest child?
At your next birthday, which cake will you get? Do you know when your birthday is? Which cake shows your age right now?
Do you have any brothers or sisters that are the ages on any of these cakes? Show me.
If you were two years younger, how old would you be—and which would be your cake?

The child who is ready may enjoy recording the combinations of candles and empty holes that add up to 10.

Wooden "cakes," 4″ in diameter.
Drill for making 10 holes in each "birthday cake."
Birthday candles or small pegs to resemble candles.
Birthday cards covered with clear contact paper for ages 1 to 10.
Small container for cards.
Small container for candles.
Container for "cakes," boxed cards, and boxed "candles."

Fences

The child puts the animals into the fences. Then he records the number of each animal in each fence. For example, one may have five horses and three cows and the child would record 5 + 3 = 8.

The teacher might discuss the activity as follows: "Pretend you are a cowboy going on a round-up. How many animals will you put in this fence?"

Tell me about your work, Amalia.
How did you decide how many animals to put in each fence?
Are there any fences that have the same number of animals inside?
Which fence has fewer than six animals inside it?
How many of each kind of animals are inside this fence?
If three of these animals got away, how many would be left? What would happen if two animals broke out of their fence and got into this fence?

4" x 4" pieces of tagboard.
Popsicle sticks glued together to form fences.
Spray paint.
Small animals of two types, such as cows and horses, to be placed inside fences.
Paper and pencil.
Small container for animals.
Container for fences and boxed animals.

Vitamins

The child fills the vitamin bottles with the correct number of "vitamins." The pill bottles may be ordered from 1 through 10. After checking his work with the teacher, he puts the cup of cereal in his desk or in some other place until recess when he may eat it!

The teacher might discuss the activity as follows: "Take one of the vitamin bottles and tell me how many vitamins should be inside. Now, what about this one?"

Tell me what you did.
How many vitamins should be put inside this bottle? (If the amount inside is not the same) Count the ones inside for me, please. Is that the number you need? Can you fix it?
Which bottle has number 1 on it? Can you put it here? What number comes next as you're counting? Can you put that bottle next? Can you finish putting them in order?
Which bottle has the most vitamins?
Which bottle has more than five but less than seven vitamins?
Which bottle shows how many eyes you have? How many toes you have on one foot? On two feet?

Empty vitamin bottles or pill vials, with tops.
Marking pen and stickers for numbering the bottles.
Small sugar-coated cereals.
Small cup to hold cereal.
Container for vitamin bottles.

Note: The cereal can be kept in a covered container on the teacher's desk or some other convenient place with a supply of small cups. When the child is ready for this activity he knows where the cereal is and can get what he needs.

Dangles

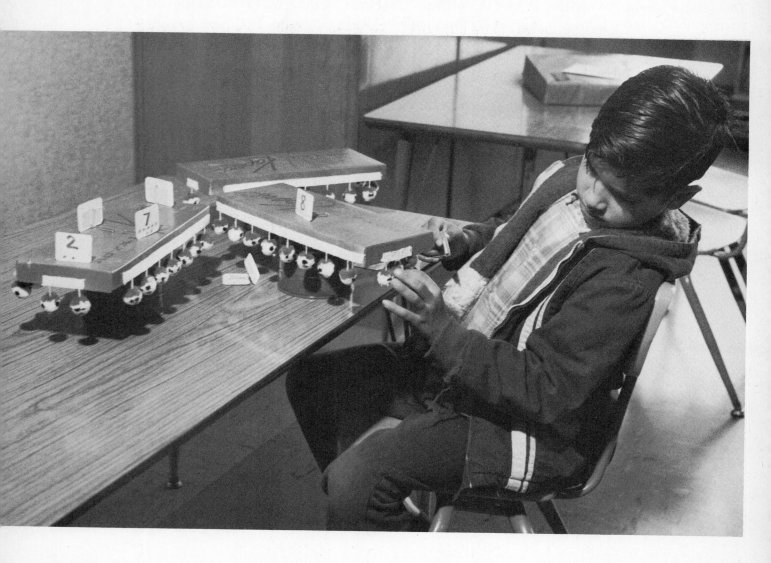

The child counts the dangles on each side of the box top and matches a numeral to them.

The teacher might ask the child, "How many dangles are there along this side? Can you find the numeral which shows that many and put it above those dangles?"

Which side of this box has the most dangles?

Which side of this box has the fewest dangles?

How many dangles are on this side? (If the child has matched the incorrect numeral with this side) Does this numeral show that many? Can you find the one which does?

Which are more, these or those? How many more are over there than over here?

How many dangles are there altogether on this top? I see a mistake on this top. Do you see it? Ask Tim if he can find it. Okay, can you fix it now?

Four tops from shoe boxes.

Four 1-lb coffee cans with plastic lids.

Four brass fasteners to secure coffee can lids to box tops.

Masking tape to tape over brass fasteners, on inside of the coffee can lid.

Spray paint.

White glue.

Lengths of dangles sold as trims in sewing or notion's departments.

Numerals, as needed, for matching to the number of dangles on each side of the box top.

Container for numerals.

Container for dangles and boxed numerals.

Note: To secure the coffee can lids invisibly to the box tops, insert the brass fastener through a small square of cardboard and then through the top of the coffee can lid. Spread the fastener open on the inside of the lid and tape over the spread. Glue the cardboard to the inside of the shoe box top with white glue.

Number Sequence

The 1-10 Train

The child hooks each car onto the train in numerical order from 1 through 10.

The teacher might discuss the activity as follows: "The engine is going to pick up its cars in order. Which one will it pick up first? Can you find that car? What car should come after that one?"

Say each number for me, please. (Looking at a car that is out of order) Let's name the numbers together and see which number should go here. One, two, three, four . . . . What number should this car have on it? Is this the right car? Can you find the one you need and hook it on? Good! And which car will go next?

Which car is between eight and ten? Which car is before four? Before seven? After two?

How many cars are yellow? Green? How many are *not* red or yellow?

Small toy engine and cars that hook together.
Black marking pen to write the numerals 1 through 10 on one side of the train car, and the appropriate number of dots on the other.
Container for toy train.

Bracelets

The child takes the bracelets one at a time, starting with number 1, and puts them on his arm in numerical order.

The teacher might ask the child, "Which number comes first when you're counting? Can you find that number on one of the bracelets and put it on? Which one will you put on next?"

Which number comes after six?

Which number is between seven and nine? (Pointing to the numeral on the numeral card and the bracelet that has been put on upside down) Is this number exactly the same as this one? Can you fix it so it looks the same?

How many bracelets are red or yellow? How many can you hold in one hand easily? How many are left over?

I am looking at an orange bracelet. What is the number on it?

I am looking at a bracelet that is between numbers three and five. What color is it?

Without peeking, can you remember the color of bracelet number ten? How about number one?

10 sturdy plastic bracelets.
Marking pen to write numerals 1 through 10 on the bracelets.
Container for bracelets.

Mach 1-10

The child takes the cars and puts them in numerical order.

ACTIVITY

The teacher might discuss the activity as follows: "Can you find Mach 1? What will come next? Can you find Mach 2? Good. What comes next?"

GETTING STARTED

How many cars are there altogether? How many cars are after Mach 8? How many before Mach 5? Which car is between Mach 4 and Mach 6? Which cars are red? Which are blue? Which ones are *not* red or blue? How many cards are as long as your arm? Your body?

IDEAS FOR
FOLLOW-UP DISCUSSION

10 racing cars cut from racing magazines.
10 labels for numbering the cars from 1 through 10.
Clear contact paper to cover the cars.
Large paper clamps (No. 1) pulled apart and taped to the back of the cars to make the cards stand up.
Container for racing car cards.

MATERIALS

Rings and Fingers

Skills Ordering numerically; strengthening left-to-right progression.

The child takes the rings one at a time and places them on the fingers of the cutout, starting at the left and working in numerical order.

The teacher might discuss the activity as follows: "The rings should go on the fingers in order. Which number will go first? And then which number?"

Tell me how you put the rings on the fingers. How did you decide which ring to put first?

How many fingers do you have? If you had one ring on each of your fingers, how many rings would you have?

Which numerals are on the left hand? Which ones are on the right?

All numbers larger than five are on which hand?

What number is on the left thumb? The right baby finger?

How many numbers are on the left hand?

(Looking at an incorrectly placed ring) Let's take these off and put them back together. Now, count which rings are already on. One, two, three, four, five, six. What comes next? Can you find that ring and put it where it goes? What number will come next?

10 small but sturdy children's rings, store-bought or made from curtain rings.
Numerals 1 through 10 attached to the rings.
Cardboard or plywood cutout of a child's hand glued to a block of wood so it will stand up.
Container for rings.
Container for hand cutout and for container of rings.

Common Objects

The child puts the items in order from 1 through 10.

The teacher might ask the child, "Can you find something that has a number 1 on it? What is this? What comes next? Can you find something with that number?"

Show me the numbers on each of the things you have put in order.
What do you do with this item? (Drink it, write with it, etc.)
(Looking at an incorrectly placed item) What number comes after ___
   when you're counting? Is this the number?
Can you find the one that goes here? Good! You fixed it by yourself.
   And what will come next?
Tell me a number on something you could eat.
Show me something you could feed a pet. What kind of a pet would eat
   that? What number is on it? Is that number more or less than five?
   Can you write that number on the board?

The following or similar items, which have a number on them and are within the child's frame of reference:

1. One-a-Day multiple vitamins
2. Ajax 2 detergent
3. Three Musketeers candy bar
4. (4) cat food
5. VO 5
6. six pack
7. 7-Up
8. V-8 vegetable juice
9. 9 Lives cat food
10. 10 Little Indians record or song

Container for objects.

Combining and Separating Groups

Ice Cream Cones

Skills Counting; combining groups; recording mathematical experience with symbols.

The child puts the scoops of ice cream on the cones. Then he records the combinations formed by the pieces of strawberry or chocolate. For example, one cone may have a scoop of chocolate ice cream with five chocolate chips. The other scoop of ice cream may have six pieces of strawberries on it. The child, in this case, records 5 + 6 = 11.

ACTIVITY

The teacher might say to the child, "Make the ice cream cones and then call me." (When the child finishes, the teacher helps the child begin his recording.)

GETTING STARTED

What did you do with the ice cream cones?

Which cones have five or more pieces of fruit or chocolate?

Do any cones have the same number of pieces on them?

Does this cone have more chocolate or more strawberry pieces on it?

What would happen if you put one more scoop of ice cream on this cone? How would you record this?

Write your favorite combination on the board without the answer, and see if a friend can give you the answer.

IDEAS FOR
FOLLOW-UP DISCUSSION

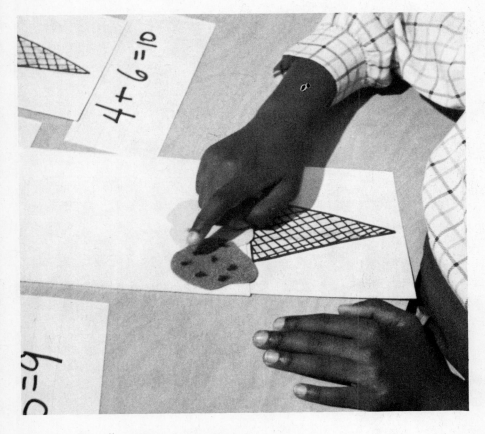

Pieces of 6″ × 9″ tagboard and cardboard.
Brown marking pen for drawing ice cream cones.
Colored felt for making ice cream and flecks of strawberry or chocolate chips.
Paper for recording combinations.
Crayon.
Container for ice cream.
Container for cards and boxed ice cream.

MATERIALS

Combining/Separating **195**

Airplanes and Hangars

Skills Counting; adding; experience with the symmetrical property of equality; matching.

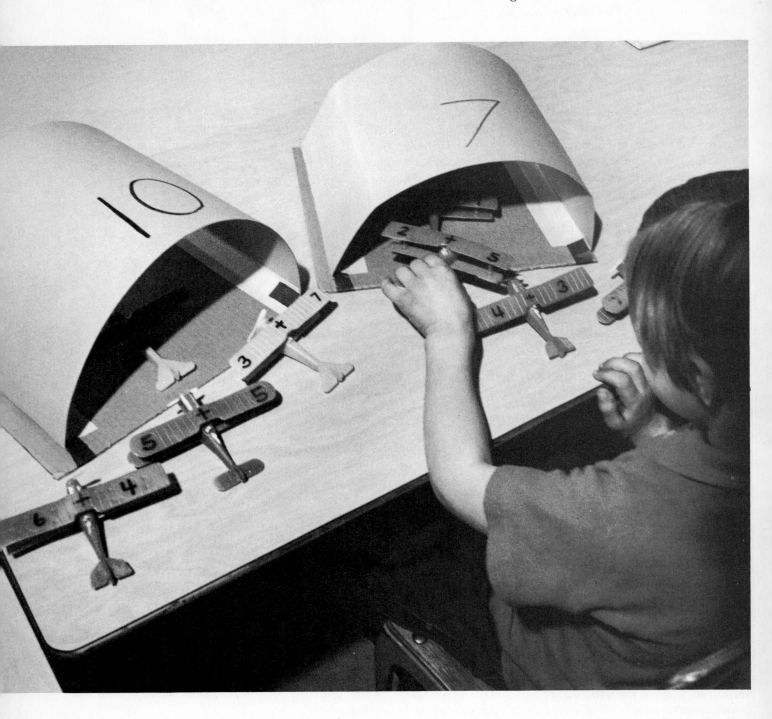

The child works out the addition problem placed on the wings and taxis each airplane into the appropriate hangar to show the answers.

The teacher may provide extra airplanes on which the child may write his own combinations with a crayon. The crayon is wiped off with a soft cloth when the child is finished.

The teacher might discuss the activity as follows: "If you add these two numbers together, how many do you get? Good for you. Howard! Can you taxi the airplane into the hangar it should go in?"

What did you do with the airplanes and hangars?
How can *both* these planes be in the same hangar?
I am looking at a hangar that has three planes inside. Each one totals seven. What colors are the planes?
I am thinking of a hangar for 4 + 1. Point to it, please.
I see an airplane in hangar 7 that doesn't belong. Can you find it and put it into its hangar?

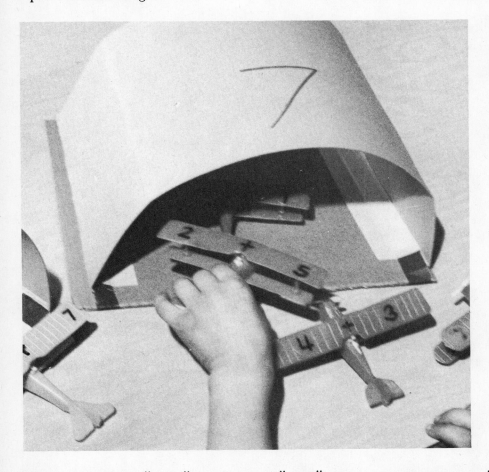

Tagboard rectangles 8″ x 18″ taped onto an 8″ x 10″ piece of cardboard to make each hangar.
Marking pen to write numerals.
Small toy airplanes with combinations written across their wing spans.
Container for airplanes.
Container for hangars and boxed airplanes.

Hide 'n' Go Seek

Skills Counting; subtracting, withdrawing a part from the whole; making abstractions; strengthening memory; recording experience with mathematical symbols.

The child decides the number he wants to work with and sets that number on the table where he can see it. He puts as many blocks into *each* pie tin as the numeral says. When he has finished, he places some of the blocks for each pie tin *under* the tin and the others on top. When a child finishes this procedure he writes on a piece of paper (placed in front of each pie tin) how many blocks he thinks are hiding underneath. For example, if a child is working with number 6 and has four blocks on top of a particular pie tin, he thinks about how many blocks must be under this pie tin since the total number of blocks is six. The child would write two. 4 + ? = 6; 4 + 2 = 6.

The teacher might discuss the activity as follows: "Select a numeral you would enjoy working with, Gina. Okay, put that many blocks into each pie tin. (When she finishes) Now put *some* blocks from this tin underneath and leave some on top. Good! Now do this for all the blocks and try to leave a different number of blocks on top of each one. (When finished) Write down a guess for how many blocks you think are under each one!"

How many blocks did you count into each pie tin?
How many blocks are there in each set—on top and underneath?
How many blocks are on top of this pie tin? How many do you think are hidden underneath? Peek and see if you're right. Were you?
Why do you think there are four blocks under this pie tin? How can you know if they're hidden and you can't count them? Is this magic?

10 pie plates from small meat or fruit pies.
1" cubes.
Paper.
Crayon.
Plastic numerals 4, 5, 6, 7, 8, and 9.
Container for numerals.
Container for cubes.
Container for pie tins, boxed numerals, and boxed cubes.

Bead Frames

Skills Separating groups; counting; learning to record experience with mathematical symbols; experience with the symmetrical property of equality.

The child separates the set of beads into two groups and records the two subsets. He matches the numerals to the bead frames that are appropriate.

The teacher might discuss the activity as follows: "Can you make two groups of beads on each bead frame? Write how many are in each group and find a numeral to put with each bead frame that tells how many beads there are altogether."

Tell me what you did with the bead frames.

Show me a bead frame that has five beads altogether. How many beads are in each group?

How many beads are over here? And how many are on this side? If you push the beads together, how many would there be altogether?

If I were to add one more bead to this group, how many beads would there be? What would happen if I took three beads away from here?

On which side of this bead frame are there more beads?

Tagboard, cardboard, and transparencies measuring 9" X 12".
Hole punch.
Shoelaces or string.
Beads.
Masking tape.
Clothespin stands made by glueing half a clothespin at the base of a complete one.
Numeral cards, hinged with dots underneath.
Cloth or tissue.
Crayon.
Container for numeral stands.
Container for bead frames and boxed numeral stands.

Bead Addition

Skills Counting; combining groups; making abstractions; learning to record experience with mathematical symbols; experience with the symmetrical property of equality.

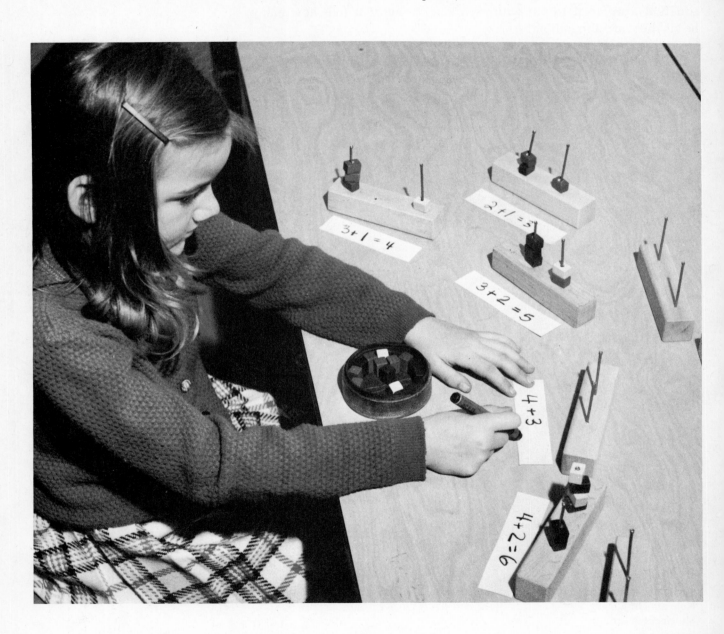

The child takes the beads and forms combinations on the nail boards. He counts to see how many he has and writes out the combinations formed. For example, a child who has five beads on the first nail and three on the second would record 5 + 3 = 8.

The teacher might say to the child. "Take some beads and put them on the nails. Then count to see how many you have on each nail and then how many altogether. Try writing it."

How many beads are on the first nail of this block? How many are on the second nail? How many altogether?

Find a block that has seven beads altogether, and tell me how many beads are on each nail.

I am looking at a block that has five beads on the first nail and two beads on the second nail. Which one is it?

There is one block that has less than four beads altogether. Which one is it?

I see a mistake on this paper. Can you find it and fix it?

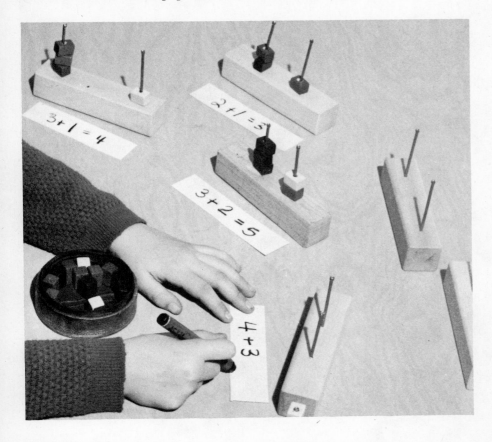

Blocks of wood.
3″ finishing nails.
Colored beads.
Paper.
Crayon.
Container for beads.
Container for blocks and container of beads.

Cars

Skills Counting; combining groups; making abstractions; learning to record experience with mathematical symbols; experience with the symmetrical property of equality.

$$2 + 4 = 6$$

$$+ 1 = 5$$

$$3 + 2 = 5$$

$$1 + 5 = 6$$

The child takes the cars one at a time and counts the dots on the wheels. He writes the combinations formed on a piece of paper. If the child has a car with one dot on one wheel and five dots on the other, he writes $1 + 5 = 6$.

The teacher might say to the child, "How many dots are there on the two tires? Can you write this down?"

What were you trying to find out?

Tell me about some of the vehicles. What are they called and what are they used for? What people use them?

Tell me about the dots on the wheels of one of the vehicles. Tell me about another one.

I see a car that has eight dots on its wheels and it is not blue. Which one is it?

I see a vehicle that men use very early in the morning; it is white. Can you tell me what it is called and how many dots it has on its wheels?

Show me a vehicle with fewer than five dots on it. What is this vehicle called? What color is it?

Show me some vehicles that have the same number of dots on their wheels.

10 vehicles—drawn, cut from magazines, or taken from sets of flannelboard vehicles.

Two black felt "tires" for each vehicle.

White crayon to make sets of dots on each tire.

Glue.

Contact paper to cover the tires after the dots have been drawn.

Flannelboard numerals and mathematical signs.

Paper and a pencil.

Container for numerals and signs.

Container for cars, boxed numerals, and signs.

Combination Blocks

Skills Counting; combining groups; learning to record experience with mathematical symbols; experience with the symmetrical property of equality.

The child forms sets with the pegs and records the combinations formed.

The teacher might say to the child, "Put a few pegs here—you don't have to fill up every hole—and some more over here. Add them up and write down how many are on each side. Try this one and I'll watch to see how you're doing."

How many are in each group of this block? How many is that altogether?

Show me a block that has ten altogether. Without looking, how many pegs would have to be in each group? Look and see if you were right.

I'm looking at a block that has seven altogether. The first group of pegs has four—how many pegs are in the second group?

Show me two blocks that have the same total. Are the groups of these two blocks the same? If not, how can they still add up to the same number?

Blocks of wood, 3-1/2″ X 8″.
Drill to make holes for pegs.
Spray paint in two colors.
Pegs.
Paper and a pencil.
Container for pegs.
Container for blocks and boxed pegs.

Snowmen

208 *Mathematics*

The child arranges a snowman on each flannelboard. Then he counts the number of buttons and writes the combination. When he has finished, the child erases the crayon from the recording sheet before putting the activity away.

The teacher might say to the child, "Make some snowmen with these parts. (Later) Write down the number of buttons beside each part of the snowmen. Under the line you can write how many there are altogether."

Tell me about your work. What did you do?
How many buttons does this snowman have altogether?
How many buttons are there on this first part? And how many are on this second part?
Show me a snowman that has five buttons on his tummy.
Show me a snowman who has more buttons on the middle part than he has on the bottom part of him.
If we took this ball of snow away from this snowman, what would you change the number to in order to show how many buttons he has?

Individual flannelboards, 6″ x 9″.
White felt for snowmen.
Compass for drawing circles.
Clear contact paper to cover snowmen.
Black crayon for making dots.
9″ x 4″ pieces of tagboard and transparency.
Masking tape to strengthen edges.
Container for snowmen parts.
Container for flannelboards, boxed snowmen, and transparencies.

Note: Cut the snowmen's bodies out of white felt. Draw the "buttons" with the crayon and cover with clear contact paper.

The Beans

Skills Counting; learning to record experience with mathematical symbols; experience with the symmetrical property of equality; subtracting, withdrawing a part from the whole.

The child determines how many beans he wishes to remove from each bunch. After removing them, he counts to see how many are left and records the operation. When he has finished, the child replaces the beans on the vine before putting the boards away.

The teacher might discuss the activity as follows: "How many beans would you like to take away from this bunch? Okay. How many do you think will be left? Try it and see. Were you right? Good. Can you write what you did?"

How many beans did you have to start with here? And how many are there now? What happened in between? How many did you take off? If you put them back on, how many would you have? Show me.
Which group has the most beans on the vine? Which has the least?
How many beans did you take away from here? And here?
Is there any place where you took all the beans off? What would happen if you did? How many would be left?
How many beans would be left if you removed zero beans from this group? How can that be?

Plastic beans whose pods can be easily removed and replaced on the stem.
6″ x 9″ pieces of 1/8″ plywood on which the beans are secured with heavy staples.
Paper and pencil.
Container for the bean boards.

Relationships

The Cylinders

The child takes the graduated cardboard tubes and experiments until he has the pieces in an orderly, progressive row.

The child should be allowed to experiment to find the best system, for him, for getting the tubes into the desired arrangement. A child with little experience will usually begin haphazardly in the middle and work toward both ends. This same child will soon begin to work from one end, judging with his eye and predicting which cylinder goes next in the series. Each child should be allowed to gain this insight through his own experience.

The teacher, pointing to the reference card, might say, "Arrange the cylinders to look like this pattern."

How did you line the cylinders up?

Which cylinder is the tallest? Is it on the right or left side?

If I take this cylinder away, which one is the tallest? If I take this one away too, is it still the tallest?

How can you make this cylinder the shortest in a series without cutting it shorter?

Can you mix the cylinders up and work backwards, so the little one is on the other side?

Close your eyes. I'm going to do something, and I want you to tell me where the pattern is broken. (Teacher removes a cylinder leaving the others in place. The child points to the space. The teacher repeats but closes the space up. Finally she does it and mixes up the cylinders to the child must rebuild the pattern to find which one is missing.)

Cardboard tubing cut into 1/2" graduated pieces.
Spray paint.
Container for cylinders.
Reference card, glued to container which shows gradation.

Syrup Game

Skills Making comparisons; observing the relationship of one size to another; ordering by size; making selections; developing visual perception; making and checking predictions.

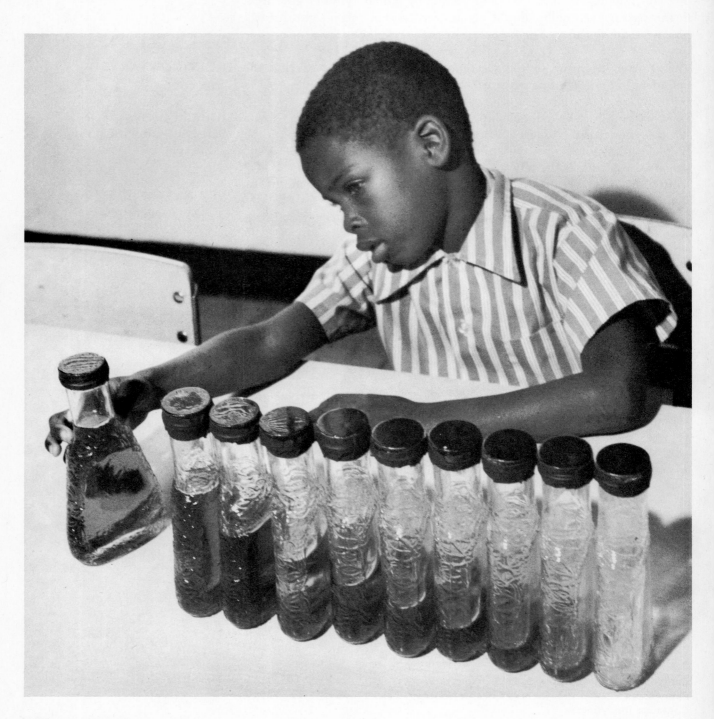

A child takes the bottles of colored water, which have been filled at 1/2" gradations, and lines them up in order.

The teacher might discuss the activity as follows: "Do you remember the cardboard cylinder game, Tim? This is a lot like that game. Will you arrange these bottles in the same order?"

What can you tell me about the bottles?

If you had all your relatives over to breakfast next Sunday, which bottle would you want to have on the table filled with syrup? Why?

If you were going to have pancakes after school and you were the only one that was going to have them, which size would you choose to be filled with syrup? Why?

Which bottle has the least amount in it? The most? How many are in between? Which ones would you say have a lot? Which ones would you say have just a little bit?

Empty bottles.
Colored water in increasing amounts in each bottle.
Cloth tape to seal bottles.
Tall container for bottles to prevent them from tipping over.

Measuring Game

Skills Making comparisons; observing the relationship of one size to another; counting; developing visual perception; estimating; measuring; gathering simple data; learning about area.

The child chooses various objects to measure which are about ___ feet long (a length chosen by the child). For example, if he chooses to measure things about five feet long, he finds five things which are about this length and draws a picture of each.

Children should measure many things with *their* feet, their hands, a book, or toys before doing this workjob. For example, one child might measure a table and find it "four spelling books long." Another child might measure the same table and find it "fifteen hands-spread-out long." Still another child might measure the table as "three toy airplane wings long." Through this kind of experience and recording, children gradually become aware of the need for standard measurement.

The teacher might discuss the activity as follows: "How long are the things you would like to measure? Write down how long the things you are going to measure will be. Good. Now, find some things and draw pictures of them."

Tell me about your work and the things you measured.
How many things did you find that were ___ feet long?
What part of each object did you measure?
Do you think this box is more or less than ___ feet long?
How about this book? The rug? How about *you*?

10 to 20 feet (exactly 12″ long) cut from cardboard.
Paint.
Glue.
Rulers, if desired.
Container for "foot" cutouts.

How Tall Are You ?

Skills Making comparisons; observing the relationship of one size to another; counting; developing visual perception; predicting and estimating; measuring; gathering simple data and drawing conclusions.

The child measures heights and records them on the recording sheet. He writes the number of long blocks used on the long block by the child's name he measured. He writes the number of short blocks used on the short block.

The teacher might discuss the activity as follows: "Who would you like to measure first? Find out how many long and short blocks tall your friend is. Have him write his name down and write down how tall he is."

What did you find out about Gina when you measured her?
How many long blocks tall was Gina? How many long blocks was Tim? How many short blocks was Gina? And Tim? Was Tim taller or shorter than Gina? Who was shorter? Show me with your fingers how much Tim would have to grow to be as tall as Gina.

1. Tim _____ 3 7

2. Gina _____ 4 1

3. Fred _____ 3 8

2" x 8" x 14" piece of wood.
1/2" bit for drilling hole in wood for dowel.
5' of 1/2" doweling.
12 1" pieces of cardboard tubing.
Four 1' pieces of cardboard tubing.
One piece of plywood 1-1/2" x 7" with hole drilled in one end to check the height of each child's head.
Recording sheets for recording and comparing heights of children.
Container for cardboard tubing.

Graphing Game

In consultation with the teacher, the child decides what he is going to survey (how many children have on black shoes, or how many have on brown shoes; who is absent, or who is present; who has a dog for a pet, or who has a cat; who has lost a tooth in the front of his mouth, or who hasn't). The child draws a picture of each category and places them at the top of the graphing chart. Then he does the survey of the class and pins each picture on the appropriate side.

The teacher might discuss the activity in this way, "Think of something you would like to know about our class." (Later) "Draw a picture of these two things and then ask each person in class what his or her opinion is. Then pin his picture under his opinion."

What did you find out?
How many children are there altogether in our class?
How many boys are in our class? How many girls?
Which group in your survey had the most in it? What does that mean?
Where did you put *yourself*? How many boys were in the group that had the most in it? How many girls? Were there more boys or more girls in this group?

10″ x 24″ piece of cardboard.
1″ x 10″ strips of construction paper in two colors.
Rubber cement.
Clear contact paper to protect graphing chart.
Small pictures of each child cut from a group photo glued to 1″ x 2″ piece of cardboard and then to a spring-type clothespin.
Container for clothespin pictures.

The Money Game

Skills Making comparisons; observing the relationship of one quantity to another; counting; identifying common coins; identifying equivalent coin values; developing a respect for property.

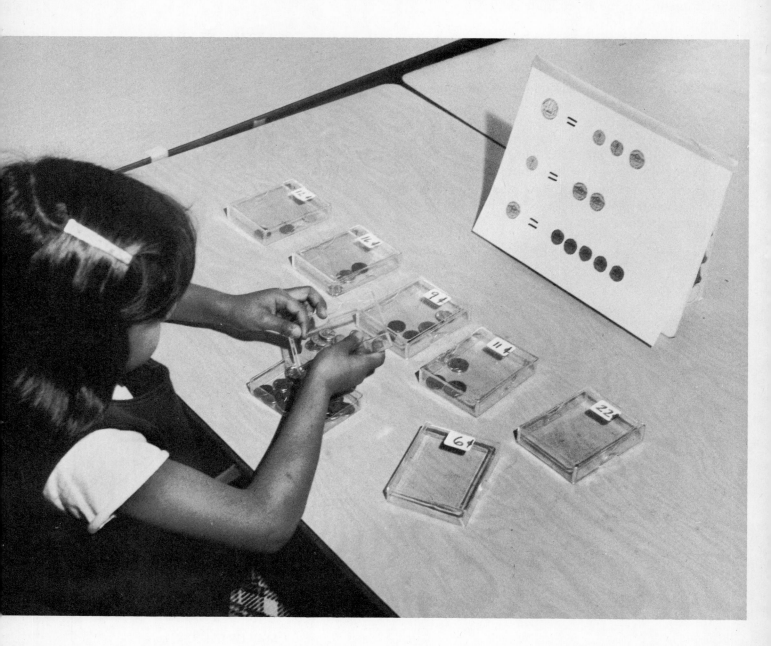

The child places the appropriate number of coins into each box. When he has finished, the child matches the silver coins to a matching board and places the pennies in a plastic cylinder. He shows it to the "loan officer" who puts it away.

Children will create different combinations. Some children working with the eleven cent box, for example, will put in two nickles and one penny, while another child will put in one dime and one penny. Still another child will use 11 pennies. It is very interesting to notice how children solve the problem when they near the end of the workjob with perhaps only two boxes left to fill and find they have only silver coins to fill a three cent and a nine cent box.

The teacher might ask the child, "How many cents go into this box? Can you count out that much?"

Tell me about the money boxes, Charles.
Which coin do we call a nickel? How many cents is it worth? Which is a dime? How many cents is it worth? Without looking, can you remember which is larger, a nickel or a dime? Which is worth more?
Tell me about the coins in this box.
Which box has the most money in it? Which one has the most pennies? Is it worth the most—could you buy more with the money in this box than with the money in any other?

Small boxes.
Marking pen for writing amounts of money.
Labels.
Real or play money.
Container for money.
Container for boxes.
Reference card showing equivalent coin values.

Note: See text at the end of the book for a discussion of the use of real money as opposed to play money (or disks) in the workjobs.

The Store

The child matches the money with the objects on the answerboard according to the amount needed to buy each item. When he has finished, the child calls the "loan officer" to put away the money squares, leaving them on the answerboard until they have been checked.

The teacher might ask the child, "If you were going to buy this package of gum, how much money would you need to pay for it? Do you have a card with that much money on it? Where will you put it? How about the car?"

Tell me what you did with all the money squares.

How many things are there to buy on the answerboard? How many things are toys? How many are things you could eat? How many are red or yellow? How much money do you need to buy this apple? How many nickels is that? How many pennies?

Tell me about the coins on the money square by the candy. How about the coins for the hamburger?

Which ice cream cone could you afford to buy if you only had 10 cents?

How many things are there to buy for less than a nickel? How many things cost exactly 7 cents? How many things cost more than 10 cents?

18″ x 24″ tagboard and cardboard.
Pictures of objects which children would like to buy in the store.
Marking pen to write numerals.
Tags on which to write each item's price.
Real or toy money glued to 3″ squares of cardboard and covered with clear contact paper.
Masking tape for taping the edges.
Container for money squares.
Reference card showing equivalent coin values.

Note: See text at the end of the book for a discussion on the use of real money as opposed to play money in the workjobs.

Time

The child places a time card beside each clock face and draws the clock's hands to indicate the time on the card.

The teacher may want to draw the minute hand on the clocks for the children who are just beginning to work with telling time. Children who are ready to work with half hours or quarter hours can be given a set of cards with these times to write.

The teacher might discuss the activity as follows: "What time does this say? Where is that number on the clock? Can you draw the short hand to that number on the clock face? Good job! Do the same for all the times."

What time does this say? Where is the long hand? Where is the short hand?

Which clock shows the time when we come to school? Which one shows when we go home? If you're not sure, why don't you keep the time board here on the counter until we're ready to go home? Then you'll be able to show me, won't you?

Can you put the time card that shows 5:00 in my pocket. Show me what time it is when we go to lunch. Show me the clock that tells what time it is now.

A clock stamp or materials with which to draw clock faces.
4″ squares of tagboard, cardboard, and transparency.
Masking tape for masking edges.
2″ x 6″ strips of tagboard.
Marking pen with which to draw times.
Clear contact paper.
Container for time cards and clocks.

MATERIALS

Shapes

Skills Learning about area; estimating; predicting; counting; developing visual perception.

The child predicts how many objects (of identical size) will fit into a particular shape and writes that number on a piece of paper. Then the child performs the experiment and sees how close his prediction is.

The size of the number is controlled by the size of the outline the child is to fill in and by the size of the objects he uses.

ACTIVITY

The teacher might discuss the activity as follows: "How many juice cans do you think will fit inside this outline? Okay, why don't you write that on the answer card and when you've put the cans inside you can see how close your guess was."

GETTING STARTED

What did you learn as you were working here?
How many cans did you think it would take to fill this shape? How many cans *did* it take? Was your guess close?
Did it take more cans or fewer cans than you guessed to fill this shape?
Draw a shape on a piece of paper, and guess how many cans it will take to fill up your shape? Fill up your shape and see how close you are.

IDEAS FOR FOLLOW-UP DISCUSSION

Large shapes cut from plywood or heavy cardboard.
30 to 40 objects of identical size: blocks, tin cans, or boxes.
Paper.
Crayons.
Container for objects and shape boards.

MATERIALS

Cups and Pitchers

Skills Making comparisons; observing the relationship of one size to another; counting; estimating; predicting; measuring.

232 *Mathematics*

The child makes a prediction of how many cups he thinks can be filled from each pitcher. He writes these predictions on a piece of paper in front of the pitchers. Then he tries the experiment and checks to see how close his prediction came to the actual number of cups each pitcher filled.

A child not yet ready to write may simply make dots or lines or pictures of cups to indicate how many cups he thinks will be filled.

The teacher might discuss the activity as follows: "How many cups do you think this pitcher will fill up? Can you write that number down on the answer card and put it in front of the pitcher? Good. Now, what do you think about the next pitcher? After you have finished, do the experiment yourself and see how close your guess is."

What did you find out?

Which pitcher could fill the most cups? Why? Which pitcher could fill the fewest cups? How many?

What about your guesses? What did you find out about each one?

Did any pitchers fill the same number of cups?

How many cups are there altogether? Are there more pitchers or more cups?

Are these two pitchers the same? How are they different? Can you tell me anything about how many cups they hold? What else can you tell me about them?

Small pitchers of various capacities (1, 2, 3, and 4 cup).
Small cups holding approximately 1/2 cup.
Rice, cornmeal, gravel, or water.
Paper.
Crayon.
Container for pitchers, cups, and pouring material.

Sharing

The child works from the teacher's directions, placing the appropriate number of biscuits by each dog.

The teacher might ask the child, "If each dog is to have three biscuits, how many biscuits will you need altogether? Show me." *Or* "How many biscuits will each dog get if you share all the biscuits among the dogs?" *Or* "How many dogs could have five biscuits each? How many dogs get none?"

Tell me what you were trying to find out. What did you discover?
Did all the dogs get the same number of biscuits?
How many dogs are there? How many biscuits did each dog get?
If you had to share the biscuits with three *more* dogs, do you think each dog would get more biscuits than he has now or fewer?

Apple crate separator.
10 pictures of dogs.
Glue.
30 small bone-shape dog biscuits.
Container for dog biscuits.

Estimating

The child puts out the jars and writes on the answer card a prediction of how many walnuts he thinks will fit inside each jar. He places each prediction in front of each jar. Then he checks his prediction by filling each jar with walnuts to see how close his prediction was.

ACTIVITY

The teacher might discuss the activity as follows: "How many walnuts do you think it will take to fill up this jar? Write the number down so we can remember it. Good. Now, can you do the same for all the jars? Then fill them up with the walnuts and see how close you came!"

GETTING STARTED

Tell me what you found out from working with the jars and walnuts.
Did you make good guesses? Did any jar surprise you with how many walnuts it held?
How many jars are there altogether?
Which jars hold a lot of walnuts? Which hold only a few?
How many jars hold less than five walnuts? Is there any jar that holds exactly seven walnuts?

IDEAS FOR FOLLOW-UP DISCUSSION

MATERIALS

Glass jars of different shapes and sizes.
A large container of walnuts.
Paper.
Crayon.
Container for glass jars and boxed walnuts.

Preschool children are creative, resourceful, and imaginative. They are fascinated with objects in the world around them—they squeeze, roll, scratch, pinch, taste, throw, pound, and chew to learn as much as they can about their world. Through this experimentation they learn that some things are soft and bounce, others are hard and break up. Some things taste good, others taste terrible. Some things are bumpy and scratchy, others are soft and smooth. Some things spread out and others stay together. Life is a fascinating world of activity to a young child—a place for doing and discovering and trying things out. Too often, however, when a child goes to school, things are different. Instead of learning in this natural way—through play, experience, and discovery—school turns out to be a place where one listens to the teacher "talk" most of the time and waits half an hour before getting his turn. A place where one watches the teacher demonstrate things on the flannelboard or listens to the teacher talk about shapes or categories or how cheese is made. School is usually where one is continually tested with dittoed worksheets and where red marks are made beside things one does not understand, where one learns to play the game of figuring out what the teacher wants for an answer, where there's a right way and a wrong way and no place for one's own way. It is a place to "hurry up" or the place for waiting when you're the first one through because there's nothing for you to do but "sit still and be quiet" until everyone "hurrying up" is finished. For most children school is a lot of stuff one has to do for no other apparent reason than that the teacher says it must be done. And for far too many children, school is a place where, for the first time in their lives, they stop learning.

Many teachers are convinced that school does not have to be like this for children. They are convinced it can be a place where every child is actively involved in his learning, where he learns in a natural and enjoyable way through his own experience. It can be a place where a child works with concepts and ideas concretely by handling familiar objects and manipulating them before dealing abstractly with the concepts on paper. School *can* be a place where children are free to make mistakes and to learn directly from these mistakes, where red check marks and "wrong" answers have no place; where errors are used, instead, as clues by the teacher to help him discover what each child, individually, needs to learn. It can be a place where a child learns to think for himself rather than play guessing games as to what the teacher wants parrotted back. It can be a place where a child learns to trust his own judgments and thoughts, where he is free to try things "his way" as an expression of his creativity and individuality. School can be a place where each child learns to work independently, where the child, rather than the teacher, takes responsibility and initiative for learning. School can be a place where a child is not told to speed up or slow down but is allowed to take his time, to work at the rhythm and pace best suited to his inner needs, where he is always allowed the pride involved in finishing his work, where he is not made to wait half an hour or half a day for a turn, but is instead actively and personally involved during the whole learning period. It can be a place where every child gains self-confidence and a feeling of worth, regardless of his ability, background, or maturity level; where he is successful at every step in the learning process. School can be a place where children move around freely and still learn; where sitting still need not be what is thought of as "good," and movement and noise as "bad." School can be a place that recognizes the talent for learning the child brings with him from home, and uses this talent to produce *more* learning for the child, not less.

HOW TO BEGIN

Theorizing is the first step in individualizing. Putting the theory into the classroom so that it works is a series of difficult next steps.

Each teacher will begin a little differently: Some will begin individualizing with one group of children and build slowly to include the entire class. Others will use an activity center for children who have finished their regular work, for children needing remedial work, or as enrichment for a select few. Still other teachers will begin the program with the entire class. Each teacher will make the appropriate workjobs to fill his particular needs.

Some teachers will want to use solely the math activities; others will use only the language activities. Still others will mix the materials, using a few from math and a few from language during the same period. Some teachers will use language activities during the first half of the year and introduce mathematics activities during the last half of the year while continuing with the language during another period.

Scheduling also will depend on the individual teacher. Some teachers will start out gradually, devoting twenty minutes and, later, an hour to activity-centered work as the children demonstrate their readiness for a longer period. Other teachers prefer a longer period, an hour-and-a-half three times a week, to allow children to become more involved. Still other teachers will feel the need to individualize the entire day and may utilize many different programs to meet this need. These teachers might choose to use workjobs in their classrooms throughout the day.

There is no "right" way nor even one "best" way of organizing the way in which the workjobs will be used in the classroom. This is entirely the teacher's decision and will vary greatly depending on many factors: the needs of the children, the individual teacher's experience in individualizing instruction, the size of the classroom, the freedom the teacher is granted by the administration and parents, the number of activities available for the children to use, and perhaps most of all, the teacher's preparation and daring.

Although the method of organizing the workjobs in the classroom varies according to each situation, there are common concerns which can be discussed to help teachers make an effective beginning. All teachers wonder how many activities to make, how to store the activities, which procedures and routines to establish, how to keep track of and assess the children's accomplishments, what the best methods are for making the activities, and so forth. The following pages contain suggestions with which a teacher can begin. As his experience grows each teacher will evolve the best method for his own class of children.

Making the Workjobs

Quantity   How many workjobs are needed to begin? A good rule of thumb is to make one and a half activities for each child who is to be included in the program. If the teacher is going to work with six children, for example, he will need about nine workjobs to begin effectively. If he is working with thirty children, he would need forty-five activities. This provides enough activities for an interesting selection for each child as he finishes one activity and is ready for another.

Strength   When making an activity a teacher should try to make it as indestructable as possible. The materials are going to be handled by young children many times each day, and they will last for many years if they are made strong at the outset. Covering all pictures, papered boxes, word cards, and so forth, with clear contact paper strengthens materials and protects them from soiling. Lamination, if available, does the same thing. Cards and games can be backed with cardboard and all edges masked to strengthen the activity and prevent bending. Taping edges of mounted pictures keeps the edges from fraying and makes them easy to shuffle so they can be mixed up at the end of each child's work with the activity.

Aesthetics Remember, each workjob is, in reality, a concept or skill in an appealing disguise. The child sees the *material*, not the concept, when he looks on the worksheet and chooses a workjob. He sees the pretty buttons, the real objects, the colored Easter eggs, or the Cocoa Puffs cereal. He wants to use these materials, so he chooses the activity. As a result of this choice, the child will experience the concept within the material. From his interest, his choice, the child almost incidentally learns. Keep this in mind when making workjobs and try to make them as appealing and tempting as possible. The goal should be to "hook" the child on the material so he can teach himself!

Classroom Organization

Teachers will find that an informal arrangement of furniture where children may work in a variety of places is most suited to an activity-centered learning program. Many teachers keep only half the desks in their room and provide cubby holes or shoe boxes for each child's storage of personal belongings. This provides much added floor space and the floor is where many young children prefer to work if allowed the choice. Be brave. Try an informal arrangement and see what it does for the children, the program, and you!

Storage

A cupboard or bookcase can be used to house the activities. Shelves should be low enough that children can clearly see all the materials from which they are to choose. Some teachers may want to label boxes

Answerboards can be placed together in a sturdy box with cardboard dividers.

and shelf areas so that the return of materials becomes a learning activity in itself. Other teachers will prefer to allow the children to figure out where there is room for their particular activity on the shelf. Some teachers may not be able to obtain cupboard space because of limited facilities or because they must share the room with another teacher, and they may even have to box and unbox the activities daily and spread them out on the counter tops.

Without the proper container the cars might be dumped into the larger box along with the garages.

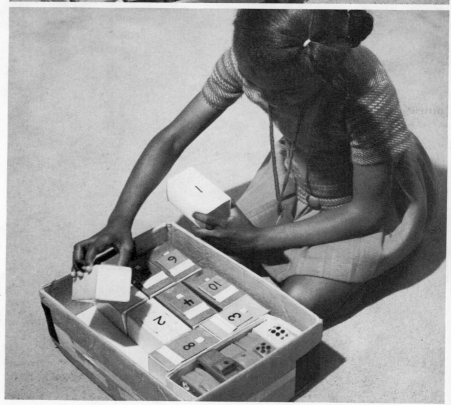

The simple addition of a box for the cars ensures the activity will be put away neatly. It is more natural to put things carefully away when there is a special place for everything.

There are several incidents which will inevitably occur in each classroom beginning to use workjobs and activity-centered learning: someone spills or breaks an activity, another puts his work away without finishing it, still another does not put the activity away neatly, and so on. These problems, if anticipated and handled decisively, will be quickly eliminated and the teacher will be free to work with the children, expanding the concepts they are experimenting with, rather than spending his time on problems that could have been foreseen and eliminated.

The following pages describe a routine designed to handle these common problems the first time they occur. Once established, this routine will help the work period run smoothly and provide the atmosphere in which real learning can take place.

The initial training period should extend over six to eight work periods. During this period the teacher is not concerned with any academics. This is a time of *learning how to learn* so that later the children can gain in real achievement. Since the teacher will concentrate during these six to eight work periods only on the children learning the routines he will want to provide work that is well within everyone's capabilities. Puzzles, lotto games, and matching activities, for example, are excellent, for they are easily taught to the children. It is important during this learning time that the children be able to do the activities with very little outside help so that the teacher is free to concentrate on the routines he must establish to ensure the program will run smoothly throughout the rest of the year.

The importance of establishing classroom routines from the start cannot be overemphasized. Once this has been accomplished, teachers will find that they can enjoy the full benefits of an individualized program throughout the rest of the year. The child's attitude about his own ability is formed during this period. He learns, regardless of his previous experience, that his teacher believes in his ability and is very interested in his way of thinking about things. He grows to think of himself as a hard worker, one who sticks to his work even if it's difficult. He feels pride in the fact that he always finishes his work and feels the freedom and responsibility he has during the worktime. He sees that he is free to move about, to select his own work, to choose where he is going to do his work. He becomes aware of his responsibility for working during the entire work period, for finishing his work, for getting help when he needs it, for telling the teacher when he is finished, and for putting away his work so it is ready for the next person who may choose it. This initial training period is a time for the teacher to lavishly praise and compliment each child to ensure his learning that he can be successful.

The basic routines that should be established during the first few workperiods are:

Selecting an activity.
Completing the selected activity.
Checking with the teacher when the activity is completed.
Putting away the activity.
Selecting another activity.

Selecting an Activity

Each child should choose his own work. He goes to the worksheet and selects an activity he would like to try. He takes the work to a table or to the floor or wherever he wishes.

Completing the Selected Activity

Each child needs to finish the work he has chosen. If the child needs help or does not know the name of an object or picture, he may ask a friend nearby to name the item. Children enjoy the idea of telling, not showing. They put their hands behind their back and help their friend "with words" rather than showing him what to do. For example, a child working with a matching game asks his friend, "Where does this go?" If the friend may not touch the workjob, he cannot take one of the pieces and put it where it goes. He must tell the child something like, "It's a bone." Through role-playing activities at some other time in the day the children can practice how they can help someone who is stuck. They will gradually understand the importance of not doing work for another child, but instead, helping him by *asking a question* that will get him to do it for himself. For example, the child above can be shown to ask his friend a question about the bone to lead him to find the place. The child might ask, "Who would use a bone?" to get him to place it by the dog.

Because the teacher is attempting to establish the fact that each person needs to finish the task he has chosen, if a child does not finish, either because he says it is too hard or because he forgets to have it checked by the teacher, he should get the task again and work on it until it is finished. This is important because at this stage the child is learning the skill of *finishing his work*. Finishing the task is how he gains the concepts he needs. If he is going to learn, he must finish the task.

Although most children view the workjobs as fun and find finishing a reward in itself, children who have been unsuccessful in the past will try a task and give up at the first difficulty. By putting it away the child is no longer frustrated. The teacher will be looking for these children during the first few work periods and will want to spend time encouraging these hesitant children, helping them see that they can finish their work and be successful.

Children who are easily distracted and whose attention span is short may be helped by playing "Beat the Clock." The teacher sets a small paper clock or an egg timer (the five-minute type obtained from drug stores) beside the child and tells him to see if he can beat the clock. He tries to have his work finished by the time the sand runs out once or twice, or by the time the classroom clock hands reach the time on the paper clock.

Lavish compliments and encouragement for such a child results in his *finishing* a task for which he may then be praised. This success and achievement is real to him, and he feels high self-esteem for the credit given to him for having done his work. Now he will try something else for which he can gain more praise and even greater self-esteem.

During this initial training period routines should be established for two situations that inevitably occur: Some things are going to spill and others will be broken. Children should understand from the beginning that it helps the teacher to know when something needs repair or replacement. When something is brought to the teacher he should thank the child and merely mention, "I can fix it." Thus, in spite of the teacher's disappointment in having to do repair work or find a new item, the children will not be afraid to bring problems of this kind to him. Because there is some unexplainable satisfaction in finishing a task and having every part present at the completion, it is important that damages be quickly repaired and losses easily recognizable. Things spilled, such as buttons or rice or blocks, should be picked up by the child and no comment made by the teacher unless it is a sympathetic observation that the child has an additional job to do.

During this period, the teacher will be watching for children who finish, and lavishly praise their accomplishment. He may even stop the class and point out particular children who are working hard and praise each one for finishing his task so well. The better the children understand that finishing their work is a praiseworthy accomplishment, the more they will strive to finish their tasks to gain this praise. *Finishing* a task becomes so routine that *not* finishing is no longer even a consideration.

Checking with the Teacher When the Activity Is Completed

During this training period, the teacher praises each child for remembering to have him check his work. What the teacher wants at this time is to make the completion of the task as rewarding as possible. He wants to establish the checking period as a time of warm, friendly, even intimate conversation between himself and the child. In time, this conversation will be the most rewarding part of the day because it is the most truly individualized time in the program, geared entirely to the needs of the individual child.

Some children will be very excited over the completion of their work and will bring their work to the teacher. The teacher should explain that, instead, he will come to the work so that things will not be spilled or disarranged. This can be established as a definite routine.

Some children will be so thrilled that they will shout across the room that they are finished and call for the teacher to come. These children should be helped to realize that they should come to the teacher's side to tell him they are finished, for he is busy working with another child and wants to give his full attention, if it is only for thirty seconds, to that child. Teachers may find it helpful to have the children role-play what would happen if everyone called from across the room at once instead of going to the teacher. The children can in this way see, through a clear example, why they should go to the teacher's side.

Children who forget to check with the teacher and put their work away during this initial learning period should rework their tasks and be reminded to check with the teacher. Some children may even forget a second time and end up spending an entire hour on the same activity the first day of the program. This may seem unnecessary, but the child who reworks his task a second time and finally remembers to have his work checked has learned the routine and will rarely forget it. Remember, the task is not redone for *today* but to establish a routine for three months from today. After all, at this stage the child is not learning to match pictures or whatever he is doing, he is learning *to get checked.*

Putting Away the Activity

This routine is twofold: The child first puts the activity into its containers (small box for individual cards, and so forth) and second returns it to the worksshelf, putting it neatly away so it is ready and appealing for the next child's use. The teacher will be looking for children who carry their activities carefully (to avoid spills) and put things away neatly. He will praise the children and may even stop the class and have everyone take notice. This boosts the ego of the child who is being complimented and makes everyone want to put his work away carefully so as to get praise. The teacher who is lavish in his compliments during this stage rarely has to remind someone later in the year to be sure to put the work away as neatly as he found it. It is very helpful to have one child stand at the worksshelf and praise those who put things away correctly during the training period.

Selecting Another Activity

The child selects another activity from the worksshelf after he returns the activity he has just finished. Later in the year, children may want to "line up" and wait for a particularly popular activity. If it is established at the beginning that the child selects his activities from the worksshelf rather than sitting beside someone finishing an activity, the children will already know the routine when this situation arises.

RECORD KEEPING   *Methods*

As the child experiences success, the *completion* of each workjob becomes self-rewarding. Beyond this satisfaction, the recording of this completion can be very enjoyable to a child. The teacher who is using the workjobs for his entire class or for one group and has individualized much of the school day will want some system of ensuring that the children are gaining the skills he has set up through the activities.

There are many ways of recording the completion of an activity and teachers will evolve their own systems as they gain experience in using the activities with their students. For teachers who wish a record-keeping system with which to begin, two methods that have proved successful are described here.

To keep track of the activities completed by each child, the teacher may glue a library book pocket to each workjob box and place a card with each child's dittoed name inside. When the child successfully completes the activity, the teacher or the child makes a small star with

a colored pencil beside the child's name. If the teacher has assembled activities that the child may do more than once, such as forming sets in mathematics, this recording system permits great freedom of choice among the activities. A child is working with *sets* regardless of whether he is putting vitamins into the bottles or putting pins into pincushions or counting objects into numbered boxes. Thus, a child who successfully masters one set activity several times will learn the concept of sets as well as another child who works with several set activities only once. For this reason, the math workjobs seem to lend themselves readily to the type of recording sheet described above.

The star-giving record has some drawbacks, however. The teacher who makes a group of activities according to certain skills that he wants to ensure the children gain will not want children to repeat the same activity over and over again. Using a separate recording sheet for each child, as shown, instead of a name card for stars, gives each child an overview of the work he has accomplished. With this recording method, each workjob is numbered, and corresponding numbers appear on the recording sheet. When the child completes a workjob and has talked with his teacher about the work, he finds the numeral on the recording sheet that matches the one on the workjob. It is extremely important that the *child,* rather than the teacher, points to the correct numeral. Even the most inexperienced child can learn to use the recording card if he is allowed to make mistakes and correct them himself. When the child finds the numeral, the teacher can make a small star with a pencil in the space and the child colors in the area to show he has finished that workjob. If the teacher is working with children who would have great difficulty finding the given numeral among fifty others, he may want to use some other symbols such as familiar shapes and pictures, or to write each row of numerals in a different color. The child would look at the *red* numeral 24 on the workjob box, for example, and then look directly to the red row of numerals on his recording card. Now he has only 10 symbols from which to select the correct one, rather than 50.

The individual recording card gives the child an immediate overview of his work, unlike the star on a card system. He can find out which workjobs he has not yet finished simply by referring to his recording card and noting which ones are not yet colored in. He keeps track of his own work. Therefore, he is competing only with himself. His work is not recorded on a single class chart where he would know at a glance if he were the slowest in the classroom. The child who *is* self-assured and enjoys competition can place his card beside that of a friend, and they can compare their progress, counting the activities they have completed, or as is usually the case, the activities they have yet to finish.

Teaching the Children to Record Their Work

During the early training period, the teacher can help the child to understand the recording activity. As with all learning, it is unrealistic to expect the children to understand the purpose or procedure of recording by listening to directions. The children will learn by *doing*. They can be given a practice card with about ten activity spaces. As each child completes an activity, he colors in the appropriate square. Most children will see the association between the numeral on the card and the corresponding workjob numeral. During this practice session, the teacher can assist the children to whom this association is not readily apparent. Children who are confused often color in *all* the squares after completing one workjob. These children can be asked if they have *done* these workjobs and can be helped to see the square they should have colored on a new card where they can start again. If the child, and not the teacher, has found the symbols or numerals on the workjob and then on the recording card, he will learn very quickly how to record his own work. Occasionally, a child who clearly understands how to record will nevertheless color some or all his squares in without having done the work. This can easily be handled by explaining to the child again the purpose of the record card, and that since he has colored extra squares neither he nor the teacher can tell what work has been completed. Because it is impossible to tell what work has been done, the child must begin all over again with a new card. The teacher will want to watch for this problem for it indicates that the child feels insecure in the routine and will need encouragement and attention for a time.

USING MONEY IN THE WORKJOBS

Teachers may feel that using real money in the workjobs presents too great a temptation to some children and that play money is just as good without the difficulties. However, most teachers feel quite differently when they have tried both play money and real money in the same activity. Not only is the realism of the activity enhanced, but teachers who try real money usually find that the responsibility the children learn is, of itself, worth the added effort. Children will respect money, for even though they would like to have it to spend, they know it really belongs to the class and is to help them learn. The children will guard the money and take great pride in the respect accorded them by the teacher in providing the opportunity to choose whether they want to use real or play money. They learn many valuable lessons if they earn the money themselves, selling cupcakes or collecting soft drink bottles, and if the responsibility for keeping track of the money is theirs. One child may be selected by the class to act as the money lender for a certain period of time. It is the money lender's responsibility to give the money bag to each child needing it and to check the money at the end of the workjob. If there is a shortage, the money lender deals with the problem.

Plastic coin cylinders can be marked to show the level of pennies or other coins. This is an excellent way for the money lender to quickly check the coins.

INTRODUCING A NEW WORKJOB TO THE CLASS

Throughout the year as the teacher makes new activities to replace or add to others, he will want to show the class the new activity before the work time begins and explain it very briefly. At this time he mentions anything special about how it is to be put away or what he wants the children to do when working with it. He points out any parts that are weak so the children know how they can help to keep the activity from becoming damaged. He impresses on the children that he made the activity for *them*. The children's knowledge of some of the intimate details of making a particular workjob often encourages them to be careful with the activities and engenders an appreciation of the fact that their teacher took the time to make the materials. The children love hearing that their teacher had a hard time finding some particular item and then finally found it at such-and-such a store in the neighborhood. Or that he needed 85¢ to buy some special thing for a workjob and had to ask if it was okay to raid the family changebox to get the money. Children appreciate their teacher's problems in making an activity, such as how he couldn't get it to stand up, or that he ran out of paint in the middle of painting the activity. These details make the activity very personal to the children and help to build a feeling in the classroom that *teacher cares*!

Index of Skills